Using Dollars and Sense

Charles H. Kahn
J. Bradley Hanna

GLOBE FEARON

Globe Fearon Educational Publisher
A Division of Simon & Schuster
Upper Saddle River, New Jersey

PACEMAKER® PRACTICAL ARITHMETIC SERIES
Money Makes Sense
Using Dollars and Sense
Working Makes Sense
Buying with Sense

CONTENTS

Director Editorial and Marketing, Special Education: Diane Galen
Marketing Manager: Susan McLaughlin
Assistant Marketing Manager: Donna Frasco
Executive Editor: Joan Carrafiello
Senior Editor: Stephanie Petron Cahill
Contributing Editors: Jennifer McCarthy, Renee Beach
Editorial Assistant: Brian Hawkes
Production Director: Kurt Scherwatzky
Production Editor: John Roberts
Art Supervision: Pat Smythe
Cover Design: A Good Thing Inc.
Interior Design: Thompson Steele Production Services
Electronic Page Production: Thompson Steele Production Services
Illustrators: Thompson Steele Production Services, Teresa Camozzi,
        and Sam Masami Daijogo

Printed in the United States of America

   4 5 6 7 8 9 10   00 99

ISBN 0-8359-3469-1

Money makes sense when you know all the coins and bills of the United States. Most people use dollars and cents every day. When you count coins and bills and add money, you are using *addition*. But you also need to learn about using *subtraction, multiplication,* and *division* with money. It will help you find out more about using money in your everyday life.

- You will learn how to figure change when you buy or sell something. This is *subtraction*.

  - You will learn how to figure costs quickly when you buy more than one of the same item. This is *multiplication*.

    - You will learn how to find the cost of one or more items when you know the price for a larger quantity. This is *division*.

While you are learning subtraction, multiplication, and division, you will also learn how to shop wisely. You will find out how to get the most for your money when you shop.

penny *or* one cent

$ .01 *or* 1¢

nickel *or* five cents

$ .05 *or* 5¢

dime *or* ten cents

$ .10 *or* 10¢

quarter *or* twenty-five cents

$ .25 *or* 25¢

half-dollar *or* fifty cents

$ .50 *or* 50¢

dollar *or* one dollar

$1.00

NAME _____

You are paying the prices in the first column. In each exercise, circle the amount of money you will use.

Price   Pay With

1.   31¢

2.   68¢

3.   75¢

4. $1.11

5. $1.75

You are paying the prices in the first column. You have the money shown in the second column. Figure out how much more money you will need. Write that amount in the blank.

	Price	You Have	You Need
6.	82¢		$ ____ . ____
7.	$1.40		$ ____ . ____
8.	$1.25		$ ____ . ____
9.	$3.65		$ ____ . ____
10.	$8.95		$ ____ . ____

Pretest II

You are paying the prices in the first column with the money shown in the second column. Figure out your correct change—the money you should get back. Write the total amount of your change in the blank.

Price	Pay With	Your Change

1.   34¢

$ ___.___

2.   89¢

$ ___.___

3. $3.75

$ ___.___

4. $7.19

$ ___.___

5. $19.98

$ ___.___

Circle the group of money that shows the correct change.

	Price	Pay With	Circle the Correct Change

6. 38¢ 50¢

7. $2.42 $2.50

8. $4.66 $5.00

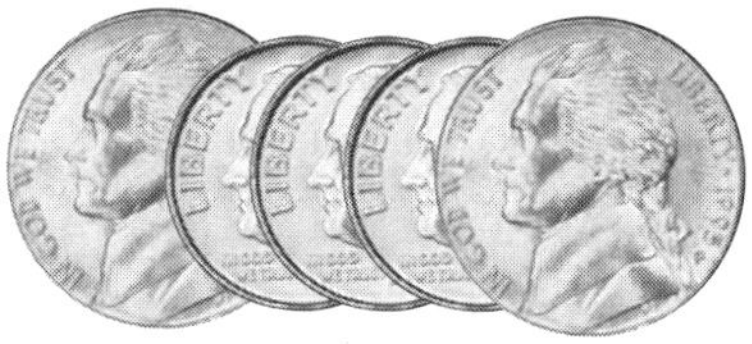

9. $9.55 $10.00

10. $19.26 $20.00

Paper money has been used regularly in the United States for only about a hundred years. Bills became popular because they are much easier to handle in large amounts than coins are. In everyday life, you will be working with large sums of money. This means that you must become familiar with the bills of the United States.

The bills you use most often are the one-dollar, five-dollar, ten-dollar, and twenty-dollar bills. But there are also two-dollar, fifty-dollar, and hundred-dollar bills. There are even larger bills than this—as much as a hundred-thousand-dollar bill! But such large bills are usually used only by banks, big businesses, and the government.

Paper money is printed by the Bureau of Engraving and Printing, in Washington, D.C. On each bill is printed how much the bill is worth in dollars. On the front of each bill is a picture of a famous American. There is another picture on the back of each bill. Each bill has its own serial number printed on the front side. You will never find two serial numbers that are exactly the same. What other things are printed on our paper money?

The bills of the United States have looked the same since 1929. In 1996, the Bureau of Engraving and Printing issued a new $100 bill. There are plans to redesign the fifty-, twenty-, ten-, and five-dollar bills before the year 2000. The new bills will be the same size and color and will have the same pictures on them.

These are the United States bills you use most often.

one dollar

$1.00

$1

George Washington's picture is on the front.

The back shows the Great Seal of the United States.

five dollars

$5.00

$5

Abraham Lincoln's picture is on the front.

The back shows the Lincoln Memorial in Washington, D.C.

ten dollars

$10.00

$10

Alexander Hamilton's picture is on the front.

The back shows the Treasury Building in Washington, D.C.

twenty dollars

$20.00

$20

Andrew Jackson's picture is on the front.

The back shows the White House in Washington, D.C.

Washington, Lincoln, and Jackson were all presidents of the United States. Do you know who Hamilton was? Do you know whose pictures are printed on the other bills of the United States?

Matching Money

Draw lines between the amounts of money that
are the same.

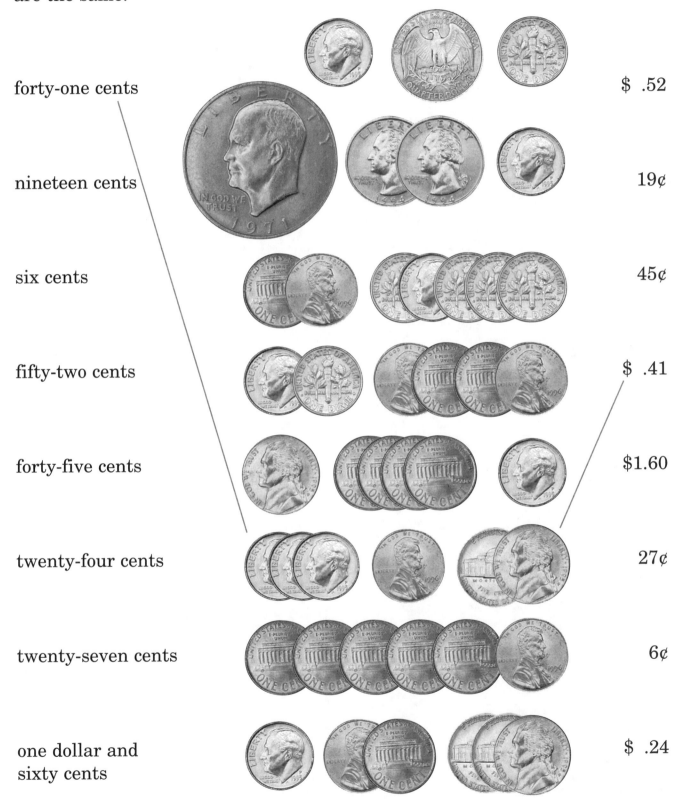

forty-one cents

nineteen cents

six cents

fifty-two cents

forty-five cents

twenty-four cents

twenty-seven cents

one dollar and
sixty cents

$ .52

19¢

45¢

$ .41

$1.60

27¢

6¢

$ .24

Write the total value of the money in each exercise
in the blanks.

1.

$ _____ 116 (with . between)

2.

$ _____.

3.

$ _____.

4.

$ _____.

5.

$ _____.

6.

$ _____.

Which Is Worth More?

There are two amounts of money in each of these exercises. One amount is worth more than the other. Make an X in the blank under the greater amount in each exercise.

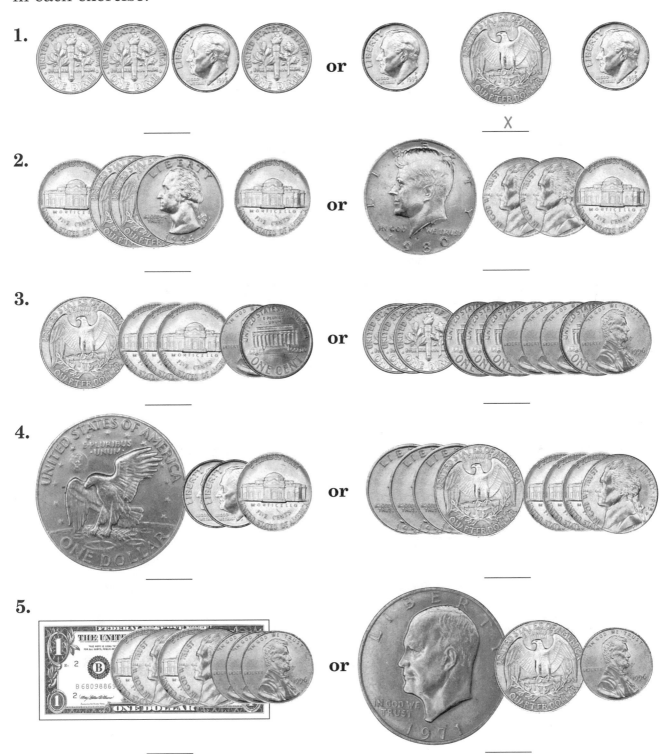

1. _____   _____X

2. _____   _____

3. _____   _____

4. _____   _____

5. _____   _____

6.  or

_____ _____

7.  or

_____ _____

8.  or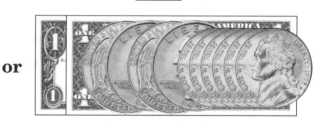

_____ _____

9.  or

_____ _____

10.  or

_____ _____

Shopping Quiz

In these exercises, you are buying different things in a grocery store. Make X's under the coins and bills you will use to pay for your purchases.

1. You are buying  — $ .82

You pay with

    X   X   X   X   __   X   X   X

2. You are buying — $ .89

You pay with

3. You are buying — 74¢

You pay with

4. You are buying — 75¢

You pay with

5. You are buying  $3.02

You pay with

_____

6. You are buying $1.80

You pay with

_____

7. You are buying $2.98

You pay with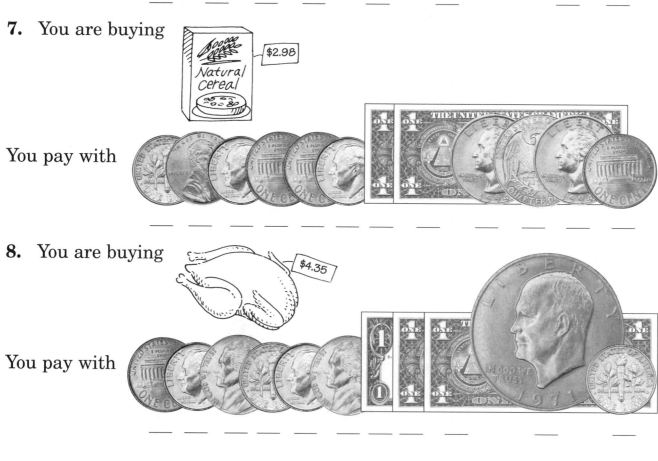

_____

8. You are buying $4.35

You pay with

_____

NAME _____

In these exercises, you are buying different things in a drugstore. Make X's under the coins and bills you will use to pay for your purchases.

1. You are buying ____ SOAP *Bath Size* — $ .79

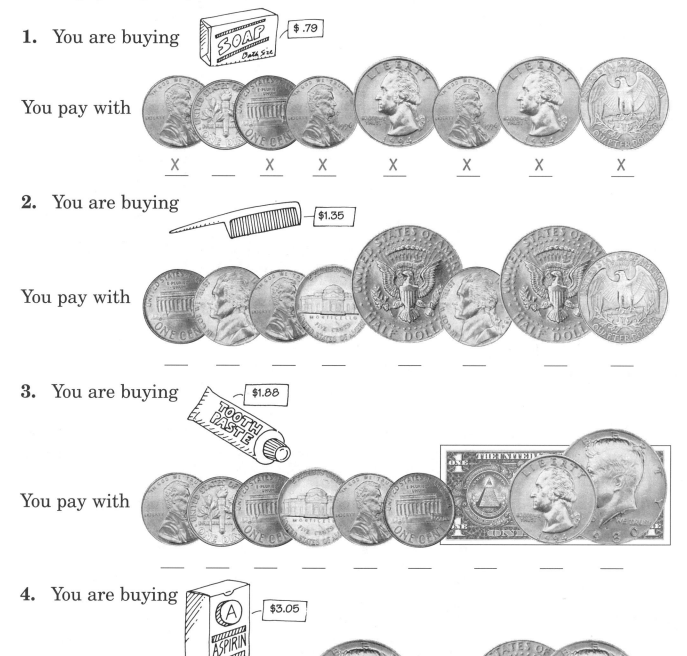

You pay with

   X   X   X   X   X   X   X

2. You are buying ____ comb — $1.35

You pay with

____ ____ ____ ____ ____ ____

3. You are buying ____ TOOTH PASTE — $1.88

You pay with

____ ____ ____ ____ ____ ____

4. You are buying ____ ASPIRIN — $3.05

You pay with

____ ____ ____ ____ ____ ____

5. You are buying

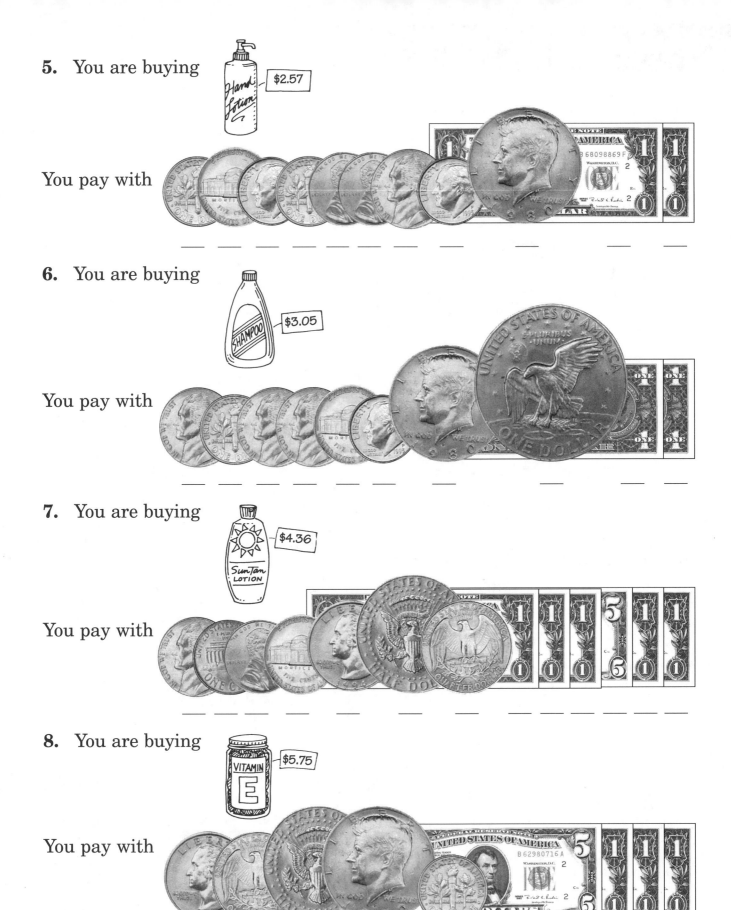

$2.57

You pay with

_____

6. You are buying

$3.05

You pay with

_____

7. You are buying

$4.36

You pay with

_____

8. You are buying

$5.75

You pay with

_____

Shopping Quiz

In these exercises, you are buying different things in a department store. Make X's under the coins and bills you will use to pay for your purchases.

1. You are buying $4.95

You pay with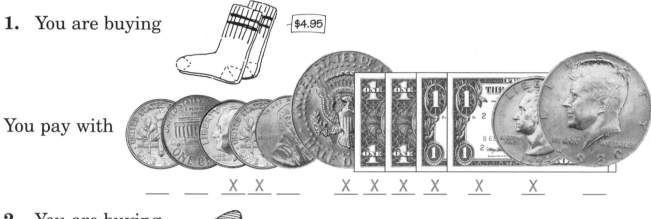

___ ___ X X ___ X X X X X X ___

2. You are buying $5.62

You pay with

3. You are buying $8.50

You pay with

4. You are buying $5.35

You pay with

5. You are buying

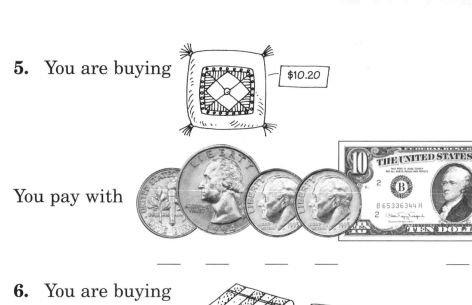

$10.20

You pay with

—— —— —— —— ——

6. You are buying

$14.05

You pay with

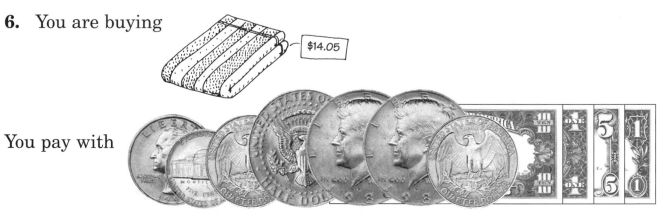

—— —— —— —— ——

7. You are buying

$21.25

You pay with

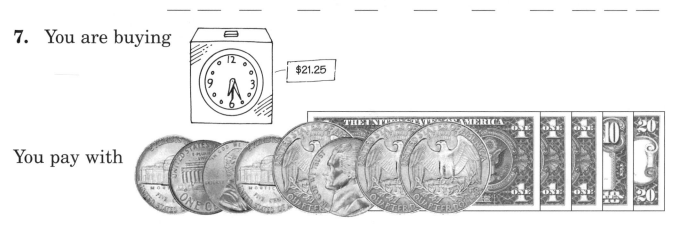

—— —— —— —— ——

8. You are buying

$22.30

You pay with

—— —— —— —— ——

Adding Money

Whenever you add money and use decimal points, you must line up the decimal points. All the money to the left of a decimal point is dollars. The money to the right of a decimal point is cents. There must always be two numbers on the cents side of a decimal point.

Add up the prices of the items below and write the total cost in the blank at the bottom. After you are done, use a calculator to check your answers.

```
$  .79        $  3.25
   5.20          28.71
  12.09          14.39
 -------        --------
$18.08        $46.35
```

1.

$3.43

$5.25

$2.99

$ __11.67__

2.

$7.40

$3.14

$1.59

$ ___.___

3.

$13.95

$3.45

$5.59

$ ___.___

4.

$28.75

$4.65

$5.23

$ ___.___

5.

$4.69

$17.69

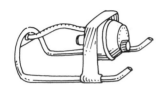

$14.95

$ _____ . _____

6.

$18.00

$4.36

$14.05

$ _____ . _____

7.

$1.97

$3.97

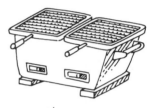

$16.25

$ _____ . _____

8.

$26.98

$2.09

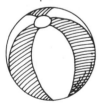

$2.25

$ _____ . _____

9.

$31.20

$19.98

$1.50

$ _____ . _____

10.

$32.95

$18.70

$6.29

$ _____ . _____

Addition in Action

Find the sums of these addition problems.

1. $ .03
   .06
   $ .09

2. $ .08
   .03

3. $ .34
   .45

4. $ .79
   .18

5. $ .52
   .27

6. 10¢
   5¢

7. 12¢
   19¢

8. 65¢
   16¢

9. 8¢
   19¢

10. 20¢
    77¢

11. $ .98
    .13
    $ 1.11

12. $ .77
    .25

13. $ .35
    .89

14. $ .64
    .76

15. $ .91
    .54

16. $ 1.45
    .93
    .70

17. $ 4.04
    .39
    1.88

18. $ 3.19
    1.66
    .25

19. $ 8.52
    .21
    .29

20. $ 2.60
    1.37
    2.98

21. $11.91
    9.23
    5.77
    $26.91

22. $ 8.53
    13.01
    19.60

23. $ 4.19
    10.92
    8.88

24. $26.41
    3.78
    11.29

25. $ 7.07
    36.54
    .79

26. $21.00
    8.17
    1.23
    .05

27. $25.09
    11.62
    2.75
    1.79

28. $ 1.11
    9.31
    8.99
    4.16

29. $16.44
    2.05
    21.43
    .27

30. $22.64
    1.19
    .26
    15.05

Find the sums of these addition problems.

1. 18
    + 5
    ———
    23

2. 49
    + 12

3. 60
    + 22

4. 73
    + 59

5. 91
    + 34

6. 87
    10
    + 32

7. 16
    72
    + 66

8. 33
    49
    + 80

9. 95
    13
    + 24

10. 9
    11
    + 58

11. 15
    48
    10
    + 50

12. 74
    55
    9
    + 13

13. 8
    35
    78
    + 28

14. 43
    14
    12
    + 2

15. 26
    81
    99
    + 15

16. 124
    55
    + 299

17. 218
    19
    + 545

18. 65
    477
    + 108

19. 103
    811
    + 26

20. 189
    443
    + 228

21. 15
    102
    189
    + 88

22. 649
    760
    355
    + 5

23. 137
    901
    24
    + 166

24. 293
    58
    656
    + 300

25. 44
    276
    98
    + 11

26. 8
    337
    584
    + 216

27. 953
    20
    14
    + 362

28. 66
    192
    29
    + 223

29. 97
    44
    481
    + 707

30. 50
    630
    8
    + 100

NAME _____

In each of these exercises, you have a certain amount of money to spend. You want to buy the item shown. Figure out how much *more* money you will need to buy the item. Write this amount in the blank.

I have	I want	I need

1.

$ __.04__

2.

$ __.____

3.

$ __.____

4.

$ __.____

5.

$ __.____

I have	I want	I need

6.

$ ___ . ___

7.

$4.35

$ ___ . ___

8.

$2.95

$ ___ . ___

9.

$8.68

$ ___ . ___

10.

$4.89

$ ___ . ___

How Much Do I Need?

In each of these exercises, you have a certain amount of money to spend. You want to buy the item shown. Figure out how much *more* money you will need to buy the item. Write this amount in the blank.

I have	I want	I need

1.

$1.35

$ __.85__

2.

$2.64

$ __.___

3.

$4.25

$ __.___

4.

$8.20

$ __.___

5.

$9.55

$ __.___

	I have	**I want**	**I need**

6.

$ ____ . ____

7.

$ ____ . ____

8.

$ ____ . ____

9.

$ ____ . ____

10.

$ ____ . ____

Do I Have Enough?

Suppose you want to buy more than one item. How do you know if you have enough money? You can use addition to find the exact total of the items. You can write down the exact prices and add them up. Or, if you want to know quickly, you can "round up" the prices and add them in your head.

Let's say you want to buy a watch for $24.95 and a coin purse for $9.97. You have $36.00. Do you have enough to buy both? To find out quickly, round each number up to the nearest dollar.

$24.95 becomes $25.00 $9.97 becomes $10.00

$25.00 plus $10.00 is $35.00. With $36.00 you can buy both the watch and the coin purse.

Most often, you will round up prices in your head. In these exercises, you'll practice rounding up and adding on paper. Round up these prices to find out if you have enough to buy the following items.

(In some states sales tax is added to the total at the register. Find out about the sales tax in your state. You can get a sales tax table to help you figure your total cost.)

You want	Price (rounded up to the nearest dollar)	You have	Can you buy both?
1. $12.84 / $10.77	$13.00 / $11.00 / Total $24.00	$ 26.00	yes
2. $39.95 / $54.62	___ / ___ / Total ___	$105.00	___
3. $11.65 / $19.96	___ / ___ / Total ___	$ 30.00	___

You want	Price (rounded up to the nearest dollar)	You have	Do you have enough?

4. flip-flops $5.62, towel $14.05

Price: _____ _____ Total _____

You have: $22.50

Do you have enough? _____

5. flashlight $4.25, batteries $2.64

Price: _____ _____ Total _____

You have: $10.00

Do you have enough? _____

6. puzzle $4.49, harmonica $9.95

Price: _____ _____ Total _____

You have: $13.00

Do you have enough? _____

7. raft $45.85, binoculars $57.97

Price: _____ _____ Total _____

You have: $100.00

Do you have enough? _____

8. shirt $17.59, pants $28.65, jacket $21.95

Price: _____ _____ _____ Total _____

You have: $75.00

Do you have enough? _____

NAME _____

"Change" is the difference between the amount of money something costs and the amount of money given for it. For example, if an item costs five cents and you give a dime for it, your change will be five cents.

Everyone has to learn how to figure change correctly. You receive change almost every time you buy something. You must be sure that you are getting the right change. If you are working in a place where you handle money, you must give other people the right change. This is called "making change."

People who work in stores know how to make change quickly. Let's say you are buying an apple that costs thirty cents. You give the clerk a dollar. He gives you your change, saying:

30¢ for the apple
and **10¢** makes 40¢
and **10¢** makes 50¢
and **25¢** makes 75¢
and **25¢** makes $1

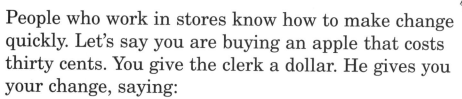

This is the change the clerk gives you.

He could also make change for you this way:

30¢ for the apple
and **10¢** makes 40¢
and **10¢** makes 50¢
and **50¢** makes $1

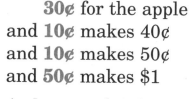

As long as the change the clerk gives you comes to 70¢, it makes no difference which coins he gives you. What other groups of coins could you get in change for your dollar?

When you count your change in a store, start with the cost of what you are buying. Then add on the money that the clerk gives you in change. Your sum should equal the amount of money you gave the clerk for your purchase. Here is another example.

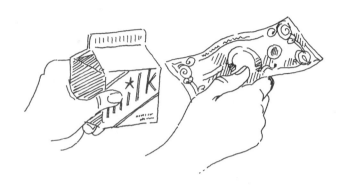

You buy a small milk for 54¢. You give the clerk a dollar. She gives you change of a penny, two dimes, and a quarter, saying:

        54¢ for the milk
and   **1¢** makes 55¢
and **10¢** makes 65¢
and **10¢** makes 75¢
and **25¢** makes $1.00

What other coins could the clerk have given you as your change? (Fill in the blanks.)

1. _1_ penny, _3_ nickels, and _3_ dimes

2. __ penny, __ nickels, and __ quarter

3. __ penny, __ nickels, and __ dime

4. __ penny, __ nickels, __ dime, and __ quarter

People who work with money must be able to figure change correctly in their heads. Here is another example of making change in a store.

You buy flower seed for $.84. You give the clerk $1.00. He gives you change of a penny, a nickel, and a dime, saying:

        $ .84 for the seeds
and **$ .01** makes $ .85
and **$ .05** makes $ .90
and **$ .10** makes $1.00

What other coins could the clerk have given you as your change?

NAME _____

In these exercises, figure your change for things that you are buying in a grocery store. Fill in the blanks with the coins you should get in change.

1. You are buying a cucumber.

Cost: 33¢
Paid: 50¢

cucumber	costs	33¢
and 1 penny	makes	34¢
and ___1 penny___	makes	35¢
and 1 dime	makes	45¢
and ___1 nickel___	makes	50¢

2. You are buying yogurt.

Cost: 87¢
Paid: $1.00

yogurt	costs	87¢
and 1 penny	makes	88¢
and _____	makes	89¢
and 1 penny	makes	90¢
and _____	makes	$1.00

3. You are buying a lemon.

Cost: 34¢
Paid: $1.00

lemon	costs	34¢
and _____	makes	35¢
and 1 nickel	makes	40¢
and _____	makes	50¢
and _____	makes	$1.00

4. You are buying celery.

Cost: 92¢
Paid: $1.00

celery	costs	92¢
and _____	makes	93¢
and _____	makes	94¢
and 1 penny	makes	95¢
and _____	makes	$1.00

5. You are buying carrots.

Cost: 39¢
Paid: $1.00

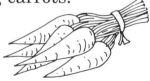

carrots	cost	39¢
and _____	makes	40¢
and _____	makes	50¢
and _____	makes	$1.00

6. You are buying eggs.

Cost: 93¢
Paid: $1.00

eggs	cost	93¢
and _____	makes	94¢
and _____	makes	95¢
and _____	makes	$1.00

In these exercises, figure your change for things that you are buying in a drugstore. Fill in the blanks to show the correct change.

7. You are buying pencils.

Cost: 84¢
Paid: $1.00

pencils		cost	84¢
and 1 penny		makes	85¢
and	1 nickel	makes	90¢
and	1 dime	makes	$1.00

8. You are buying notebook paper.

Cost: $1.38
Paid: $1.50

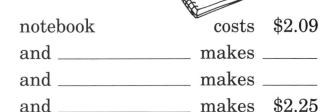

notebook paper		costs	$1.38
and 1 penny		makes	_____
and	_____	makes	_____
and	_____	makes	$1.50

9. You are buying envelopes.

Cost: $1.69
Paid: $2.00

envelopes		cost	$1.69
and	_____	makes	$1.70
and	_____	makes	_____
and	_____	makes	$2.00

10. You are buying a notebook.

Cost: $2.09
Paid: $2.25

notebook		costs	$2.09
and	_____	makes	_____
and	_____	makes	_____
and	_____	makes	$2.25

11. You are buying a birthday card.

Cost: $1.35
Paid: $5.00

card		costs	$1.35
and 1 nickel		makes	_____
and	_____	makes	$1.50
and	_____	makes	$2.00
and 1 dollar		makes	_____
and	_____	makes	_____
and	_____	makes	$5.00

12. You are buying glue.

Cost: $1.49
Paid: $5.00

glue		costs	$1.49
and	_____	makes	_____
and	_____	makes	$1.75
and	_____	makes	_____
and	_____	makes	_____
and	_____	makes	$5.00

Figuring Your Change

Figure your change for these purchases that you are making in a clothing store. Fill in the blanks to show the correct change.

1. You pay $5.00 for socks that cost $3.20.

socks		$3.20
and _1 nickel_	=	$3.25
and _1 quarter_	=	$3.50
and _1 half-dollar_	=	$4.00
and _1 dollar_	=	$5.00

2. You pay $5.00 for a hat that costs $4.63.

hat		$4.63
and _____	=	_____
and _____	=	_____
and _____	=	_____
and _____	=	$5.00

3. You pay $9.50 for a tie that costs $9.05.

tie		$9.05
and _____	=	_____
and _____	=	_____
and _____	=	$9.50

4. You pay $10.00 for baby clothes that cost $9.39.

baby clothes		$9.39
and _____	=	_____
and _____	=	_____
and _____	=	$10.00

5. You pay $10.00 for boots that cost $9.44.

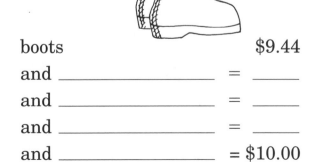

boots		$9.44
and _____	=	_____
and _____	=	_____
and _____	=	_____
and _____	=	$10.00

6. You pay $15.00 for an umbrella that costs $12.85.

umbrella		$12.85
and _____	=	_____
and _____	=	_____
and _____	=	_____
and _____	=	$15.00

7. You pay $10.00 for a belt that costs $8.38.

belt		$8.38
and _____	=	_____
and _____	=	_____
and _____	=	_____
and _____	=	_____
and _____	=	_____
and _____	= $10.00	

8. You pay $20.00 for a shirt that costs $17.59.

shirt		$17.59
and _____	=	_____
and _____	=	_____
and _____	=	_____
and _____	=	_____
and _____	=	_____
and _____	= $20.00	

9. You pay $23.00 for a blouse that costs $22.39.

blouse		$22.39
and _____	=	_____
and _____	=	_____
and _____	= $23.00	

10. You pay $30.00 for a sweater that costs $29.84.

sweater		$29.84
and _____	=	_____
and _____	=	_____
and _____	= $30.00	

11. You pay $30.00 for shoes that cost $28.40.

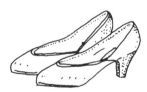

shoes		$28.40
and _____	=	_____
and _____	=	_____
and _____	= $30.00	

12. You pay $30.00 for jeans that cost $28.65.

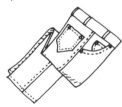

jeans		$28.65
and _____	=	_____
and _____	=	_____
and _____	= $30.00	

Figuring Your Change

Figure your change for these purchases that you are
making in a sporting goods store. Fill in the blanks to
show the correct change.

1. You pay $30.00 for a football that
costs $24.79.

$24.79

+ ___1 penny___	=	$24.80
+ ___1 dime___	=	$24.90
+ ___1 dime___	=	$25.00
+ ___1 five-dollar bill___	=	$30.00

2. You pay $35.00 for a fishing pole
that costs $33.69.

$33.69

+ _____	=	____
+ _____	=	____
+ _____	=	____
+ _____	=	$35.00

3. You pay $35.00 for a tennis racket
that costs $32.19.

$32.19

+ _____	=	____
+ _____	=	____
+ _____	=	____
+ _____	=	____
+ _____	=	____
+ _____	=	$35.00

4. You pay $35.00 for a swimsuit
that costs $31.60.

$31.60

+ _____	=	____
+ _____	=	____
+ _____	=	____
+ _____	=	____
+ _____	=	____
+ _____	=	$35.00

5. You pay $30.00 for a baseball glove
that costs $29.64.

$29.64

+ _____	=	____
+ _____	=	____
+ _____	=	$30.00

6. You pay $30.00 for a life jacket
that costs $28.94.

$28.94

+ _____	=	____
+ _____	=	____
+ _____	=	$30.00

7. You pay $30.00 for an ice chest
that costs $26.98.

$26.98

+ _____	=	____
+ _____	=	____
+ _____	=	____
+ _____	=	____
+ _____	=	$30.00

8. You pay $30.00 for a backpack
that costs $24.34.

$24.34

+ _____	=	____
+ _____	=	____
+ _____	=	____
+ _____	=	____
+ _____	=	$30.00

9. You pay $30.00 for a basketball that costs $23.79.

$23.79
+ _____ = _____
+ _____ = _____
+ _____ = _____
+ _____ = _____
+ _____ = $30.00

10. You pay $60.00 for roller blades that cost $54.38.

$54.38
+ _____ = _____
+ _____ = _____
+ _____ = _____
+ _____ = _____
+ _____ = $60.00

11. You pay $60.00 for field glasses that cost $57.97.

$57.97
+ _____ = _____
+ _____ = _____
+ _____ = _____
+ _____ = _____
+ _____ = $60.00

12. You pay $50.00 for a swimsuit that costs $44.43.

$44.43
+ _____ = _____
+ _____ = _____
+ _____ = _____
+ _____ = _____
+ _____ = $50.00

13. You pay $60.00 for a camping stove that costs $57.15.

$57.15
+ _____ = _____
+ _____ = _____
+ _____ = _____
+ _____ = _____
+ _____ = _____
+ _____ = $60.00

14. You pay $80.00 for a sleeping bag that costs $75.74.

$75.74
+ _____ = _____
+ _____ = _____
+ _____ = _____
+ _____ = _____
+ _____ = _____
+ _____ = $80.00

15. You pay $100.00 for a tent that costs $93.43.

$93.43
+ _____ = _____
+ _____ = _____
+ _____ = _____
+ _____ = _____
+ _____ = _____
+ _____ = $100.00

16. You pay $100.00 for a bicycle that costs $96.84.

$96.84
+ _____ = _____
+ _____ = _____
+ _____ = _____
+ _____ = _____
+ _____ = _____
+ _____ = $100.00

Figuring Your Change

Figure your change for these purchases that you are making in a department store. Fill in the blanks to show the correct change.

1. You pay $20.00 for a blank cassette tape that costs $4.98.

$4.98

+	1 penny	=	$4.99
+	1 penny	=	$5.00
+	1 five-dollar bill	=	$10.00
+	1 ten-dollar bill	=	$20.00

2. You pay $20.00 for a game of checkers that costs $8.70.

$8.70

+	_____	=	____
+	_____	=	____
+	_____	=	____
+	_____	=	$20.00

3. You pay $15.00 for a video tape that costs $13.43.

$13.43

+	_____	=	____
+	_____	=	____
+	_____	=	____
+	_____	=	____
+	_____	=	____
+	_____	=	$15.00

4. You pay $30.00 for a coffeemaker that costs $23.83.

$23.83

+	_____	=	____
+	_____	=	____
+	_____	=	____
+	_____	=	____
+	_____	=	____
+	_____	=	$30.00

5. You pay $20.00 for a pillow that costs $13.70.

$13.70

+	_____	=	____
+	_____	=	____
+	_____	=	____
+	_____	=	$20.00

6. You pay $20.00 for a blanket that costs $19.38.

$19.38

+	_____	=	____
+	_____	=	____
+	_____	=	____
+	_____	=	$20.00

7. You pay $20.00 for a hair dryer that costs $18.74.

$18.74

+	_____	=	____
+	_____	=	____
+	_____	=	$20.00

8. You pay $20.25 for a mirror that costs $20.19.

$20.19

+	_____	=	____
+	_____	=	$20.25

9. You pay $20.00 for a picnic basket that costs $17.46.

$17.46

+ _____ = _____
+ _____ = _____
+ _____ = _____
+ _____ = _____
+ _____ = _____
+ _____ = _____
+ _____ = $20.00

10. You pay $30.00 for a wall clock that costs $22.10.

$22.10

+ _____ = _____
+ _____ = _____
+ _____ = _____
+ _____ = _____
+ _____ = _____
+ _____ = _____
+ _____ = $30.00

11. You pay $50.00 for a lamp that costs $40.15.

$40.15

+ _____ = _____
+ _____ = _____
+ _____ = _____
+ _____ = _____
+ _____ = _____
+ _____ = _____
+ _____ = _____
+ _____ = $50.00

12. You pay $30.00 for a music box that costs $26.53.

$26.53

+ _____ = _____
+ _____ = _____
+ _____ = _____
+ _____ = _____
+ _____ = _____
+ _____ = _____
+ _____ = _____
+ _____ = $30.00

13. You pay $35.00 for a popcorn popper that costs $33.35.

$33.35

+ _____ = _____
+ _____ = _____
+ _____ = _____
+ _____ = $35.00

14. You pay $90.00 for a gold ring that costs $84.69.

$84.69

+ _____ = _____
+ _____ = _____
+ _____ = _____
+ _____ = $90.00

15. You pay $60.00 for a camera that costs $41.95.

$41.95

+ _____ = _____
+ _____ = _____
+ _____ = _____
+ _____ = _____
+ _____ = _____
+ _____ = $60.00

16. You pay $60.00 for a clock radio that costs $53.38.

$53.38

+ _____ = _____
+ _____ = _____
+ _____ = _____
+ _____ = _____
+ _____ = _____
+ _____ = $60.00

Subtracting to Figure Change

In arithmetic, figuring change is called *subtraction*. Whenever you are taking one amount out of another amount, you are subtracting. For example, you give a half-dollar for an item that costs a quarter. Your change would be twenty-five cents. On paper you would write this

$$\begin{array}{r} \$\ .50 \\ -\ .25 \\ \hline \$\ .25 \end{array}$$ or $\$\ .50 - \$\ .25 = \$\ .25$

You would read the problem above as, "Fifty cents minus twenty-five cents equals twenty-five cents."

Here are some more examples.

$$\begin{array}{r} \$5.00 \\ -3.25 \\ \hline \$1.75 \end{array}$$ $$\begin{array}{r} \$20.00 \\ -15.35 \\ \hline \$\ 4.65 \end{array}$$

Fill in the missing numbers to complete these
subtraction problems.

1.

$$\begin{array}{r} \$\ .\ 7\underline{} \\ -\ .\ 3\ 0 \\ \hline \$\ .\ \underline{}\ 5 \end{array}$$

2.

$$\begin{array}{r} \$\ .\ \underline{}\ 0 \\ -\ .\ 5\ \underline{} \\ \hline \$\ .\ 3\ 0 \end{array}$$

3.

$$\begin{array}{r} \$\ \underline{}\ .\ 0\ 0 \\ -\ .\ \underline{}\ 5 \\ \hline \$\ .\ 3\ \underline{} \end{array}$$

4.

$$\begin{array}{r} \$\ 2\ .\ \underline{}\ 5 \\ -\ 1\ .\ 2\ 2 \\ \hline \$\ \underline{}\ .\ 1\ \underline{} \end{array}$$

Subtracting to Figure Change

Subtract the amount of money on the left from the amount of money on the right. Then write the arithmetic problem in numbers. Write the amount of change in the blanks.

Subtract This Amount	From This Amount	Write the Problem and the Answer

1.

$$\begin{array}{r} \$\ .50 \\ -\ \ .40 \\ \hline \$\ .10 \end{array}$$

Your Change Is: ___$ .10___

2.

Your Change Is: _____

3.

Your Change Is: _____

4.

Your Change Is: _____

5.

Your Change Is: _____

Subtract This Amount	From This Amount	Write the Problem and the Answer

6.

Your Change Is: _____

7.

Your Change Is: _____

8.

Your Change Is: _____

9.

Your Change Is: _____

NAME _____

In these exercises, you are working as a clerk in a store. The cost of the items your customers are buying is shown in the first column. The money they pay you is shown in the second column. Write the correct change in the blanks in the third column.

Take This Amount	Out of This Amount	And Give This Change

1.

$ .25

2.

_____

3.

_____

4.

_____

5.

_____

Take This Amount	Out of This Amount	And Give This Change

6.   _____

7.   _____

8.   _____

9.   _____

10.   _____

11.   _____

12.   _____

NAME _____

Count the coins between every two spokes of the wheel.
Subtract each sum from the amount in the middle of the
wheel. Write your change in the blanks along the rim.

Change $ .98

Change _____

Change _____

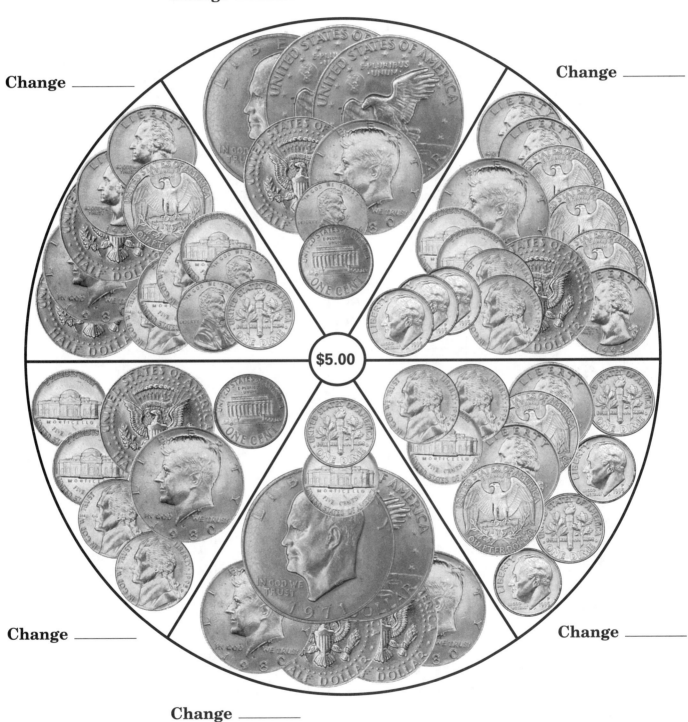

$5.00

Change _____

Change _____

Change _____

Add only the coins inside the wheel. What is the sum? _____

Start at the center and subtract each amount of money from the total amount just before it. Work through each line of coins. Write your final change in the answer boxes.

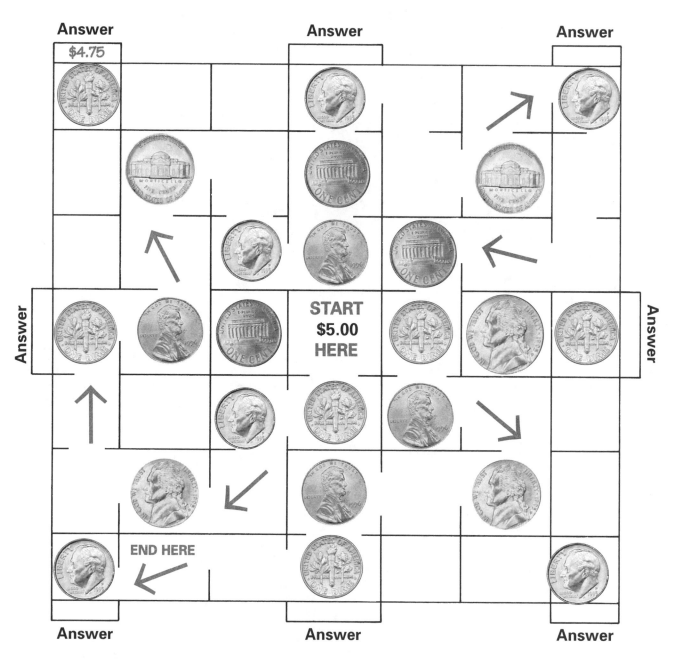

Now, to work the maze, start in the center and follow the openings through each square. As you pass through the maze, subtract each amount of money from the total amount just before it. Write your final change here: _____

NAME _____

You are buying the items in the first column with the money in the second column. Figure out your correct change and write the total amount in the blank.

You Buy	Pay With	Your Change

1.

Total change __3__ ¢

2.

Total change _____ ¢

3.

Total change _____ ¢

4.

Total change _____ ¢

You Buy	Pay With	Your Change

5.

 $1.59

Total change _____ ¢

6.

 $4.49

Total change _____ ¢

7.

 $4.88

Total change _____ ¢

8.

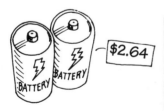 $2.64

Total change _____ ¢

NAME _____

You are buying the items in the first column with the money in the second column. Figure out your correct change and write the total amount in the blank.

You Buy	Pay With	Your Change

1.   Total change __6__ ¢

2.   Total change ____ ¢

3.   Total change ____ ¢

4.   Total change ____ ¢

5.   Total change ____ ¢

You Buy	Pay With	Your Change

6.

 $1.49

Total change ____ ¢

7.

 $4.14

Total change ____ ¢

8.

 $3.79

Total change ____ ¢

9.

$4.28

Total change ____ ¢

10.

$3.29

Total change ____ ¢

NAME _____

You are buying the items in the first column with the money in the second column. Figure out your correct change and write the total amount in the blank.

You Buy	Pay With	Your Change

1.

Total change $____.64

2.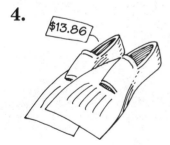

Total change $____.____

3.

Total change $____.____

4.

Total change $____.____

5.

Total change $____.____

You Buy	Pay With	Your Change

6.  $5.87

Total change $___.___

7.  $7.59

Total change $___.___

8.  $9.79

Total change $___.___

9.  $7.35

Total change $___.___

10.  $8.69

Total change $___.___

Figuring Your Change

Figure out how much change you will get back in these shopping exercises. Write the amounts in the blanks.

You Buy	Pay With	Your Change

1.  $7.52

$ _2.48_

2.  Birdseed $7.42

$ _____

3.  BIRDS $9.95

$ _____

4.  $13.31

$ _____

5.  $11.16

$ _____

You Buy	Pay With	Your Change

6.  $12.76  $_____

7.   $17.69  $_____

8.  $13.15  $_____

9.  $14.95  $_____

10.  $16.38  $_____

NAME _____

Figure out how much change you will get back in these
shopping exercises. Write the amounts in the blanks.

You Buy	Pay With	Your Change

1.   $ .21

2.   $_____

3.   $_____

4.   $_____

5.   $_____

You Buy	Pay With	Your Change

6.  $21.95

$ _____

7.  $26.75

$ _____

8.  $22.45

$ _____

9.  $33.20

$ _____

10.  $27.50

$ _____

NAME _____

Figure out how much change you will get back in these shopping exercises. Write the amounts in the blanks.

You Buy	Pay With	Your Change

1.

$ _2.05_

2.

$ _____

3.

$ _____

4.

$ _____

5.

$ _____

You Buy	Pay With	Your Change

6.  $57.97

$ _____

7.  $45.85

$ _____

8.  $44.28

$ _____

9. 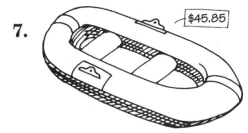 $69.43

$ _____

10.  $76.84

$ _____

Choosing Change

You are paying the prices in the first column with the money in the next column. Circle the group of money that shows your correct change.

Price	Pay With	Circle the Correct Change
1. $ .98	$1.00	
2. $1.13	$2.00	
3. $5.38	$5.50	
4. $3.74	$4.00	
5. $8.42	$8.50	

	Price	Pay With	Circle the Correct Change

6. $6.66 $7.00

7. $2.55 $3.00

8. $10.01 $10.25

9. $13.26 $14.00

10. $11.89 $12.00

NAME _____

You are paying the prices in the first column with the money in the second column. The change you are given is in the third column. If the change you are given is correct, write *Yes* in the blank following it. If you are given the wrong change, write *No* in the blank.

	Price	Pay With	Change	
1.	54¢	1 half-dollar, 1 quarter	$ .20	No
2.	60¢	6 dimes	None	_____
3.	$ .86	3 quarters, 1 dime, 1 nickel	4¢	_____
4.	23¢	2 nickels, 1 dime, 3 pennies	$ .02	_____
5.	$1.47	6 quarters	3¢	_____
6.	63¢	1 half-dollar, 3 nickels	$ .03	_____
7.	$1.13	1 dollar, 1 dime, 1 nickel	2¢	_____
8.	$2.44	2 dollars, 3 nickels, 3 dimes	4¢	_____
9.	94¢	1 half-dollar, 1 quarter, 2 dimes	$ .11	_____
10.	78¢	2 quarters, 1 half-dollar	$ .03	_____
11.	$1.82	1 dollar, 4 quarters	19¢	_____
12.	$2.39	4 half-dollars, 2 quarters	11¢	_____
13.	$4.49	5 dollars	$ .59	_____
14.	$3.50	2 dollars, 5 half-dollars	25¢	_____
15.	$5.08	4 dollars, 4 quarters, 1 dime	2¢	_____

See if you are getting the correct change in these
problems. Write *Yes* in the blank if you are.
Write *No* if you are not—and write in the correct amount.

16.   Cost of 39¢ out of $1.00 paid leaves 71¢ change.   <u>No, 61¢</u>

17.   Cost of $ .43 out of 50¢ paid leaves 7¢ change.   _____

18.   Cost of 63¢ out of one dollar paid leaves $ .36 change.   _____

19.   Cost of $1.14 out of five dollars paid leaves $4.86 change.   _____

20.   Cost of 53¢ out of $5.00 paid leaves $3.47 change.   _____

21.   Cost of $2.14 out of $2.50 paid leaves 36¢ change.   _____

22.   Cost of 98¢ out of five dollars paid leaves $3.02 change.   _____

23.   Cost of $3.99 out of five dollars paid leaves $1.01 change.   _____

24.   Cost of $1.89 out of $2.00 paid leaves 12¢ change.   _____

25.   Cost of $4.71 out of five dollars paid leaves 24¢ change.   _____

26.   Cost of $3.21 out of $4.00 paid leaves 81¢ change.   _____

27.   Cost of $5.45 out of $10.00 paid leaves $4.55 change.   _____

28.   Cost of $2.98 out of ten dollars paid leaves $8.02 change.   _____

29.   Cost of $7.36 out of $20.00 paid leaves $12.64 change.   _____

30.   Cost of $6.12 out of seven dollars paid leaves 89¢ change.   _____

31.   Cost of $10.23 out of $15.00 paid leaves $5.23 change.   _____

32.   Cost of five dollars out of $20.00 paid leaves $15.00 change.   _____

33.   Cost of $11.88 out of $15.00 paid leaves $3.22 change.   _____

34.   Cost of $19.17 out of twenty dollars paid leaves 83¢ change.   _____

35.   Cost of $48.55 out of $50.00 paid leaves $1.35 change.   _____

Write the correct change in the blank. Cross out the coins
you do not need to make the correct change in each exercise.

1. 38¢ cost out of 50¢ paid =

<u>   12¢   </u>

2. 64¢ cost out of $1.00 paid =

_____

3. 22¢ cost out of $1.00 paid =

_____

4. 71¢ cost out of $1.00 paid =

_____

5. $1.39 cost out of $1.50 paid =

_____

6. $2.40 cost out of $2.50 paid =

_____

7. $1.80 cost out of $2.00 paid =

_____

8. $3.15 cost out of $3.25 paid =

_____

9. $3.60 cost out of $5.00 paid =

_____

10. $4.79 cost out of $10.00 paid =

_____

11. $2.55 cost out of $3.00 paid =

_____

12. $1.25 cost out of $2.00 paid =

_____

Figuring Change

The cost of the item is listed in the Cost column. The coin or bill you will use to pay for the item is listed in the Paid column. Fill in the number of each coin or bill you will get in change.

	Cost	Paid	penny	nickel	dime	quarter	half-dollar	dollar
1.	58¢	$1.00	2	1	1	1		
2.	10¢	25¢						
3.	68¢	$ 1.00						
4.	77¢	$ 1.00						
5.	66¢	$ 1.00						
6.	55¢	75¢						
7.	$1.32	$ 2.00						
8.	$1.80	$ 2.00						
9.	$3.44	$ 3.50						
10.	74¢	$ 5.00						
11.	$1.39	$ 1.50						
12.	$ .63	$ 5.00						
13.	$4.40	$ 4.50						
14.	$5.90	$ 6.00						
15.	$7.30	$ 8.00						
16.	$8.40	$ 9.00						
17.	$9.32	$ 9.50						
18.	$ .72	$ 5.00						
19.	$2.89	$10.00						
20.	$ .50	$10.00						

	Cost	Paid	penny	nickel	dime	quarter	half-dollar	dollar
21.	$ .78	$ 5.00	2		2			4
22.	$ 6.72	$ 7.00						
23.	$ 1.81	$10.00						
24.	$ 2.40	$ 3.00						
25.	$ 3.50	$ 4.00						
26.	$ 5.60	$ 5.75						
27.	$ 7.20	$ 7.50						
28.	$ 8.30	$10.00						
29.	$ 6.50	$ 7.00						
30.	$ 8.30	$20.00						
31.	$ 7.02	$ 7.25						
32.	$ 5.03	$10.00						
33.	$ 6.56	$ 7.00						
34.	$16.15	$20.00						
35.	$ .87	$ 1.00						
36.	$ 2.74	$ 5.00						
37.	$18.66	$19.00						
38.	$12.18	$15.00						
39.	$ 1.33	$ 1.50						
40.	$25.88	$30.00						
41.	$ 4.69	$ 5.00						
42.	$14.27	$20.00						
43.	$49.02	$50.00						
44.	$32.45	$33.00						

NAME _____

Write the amounts of money you will receive in change.

		Cost	Paid	Change
1.		70¢	$1.00	$ .30
2.		36¢	50¢	_____
3.		49¢	$1.00	_____
4.		50¢	$1.00	_____
5.		$1.62	$1.75	_____
6.		$1.33	$1.50	_____
7.		61¢	75¢	_____
8.		$2.25	$3.00	_____
9.		25¢	25¢	_____
10.		$5.25	$5.30	_____
11.		$4.22	$4.25	_____
12.		$4.92	$5.00	_____
13.		$7.14	$7.50	_____
14.		$2.76	$10.00	_____
15.		$9.68	$9.75	_____
16.		$6.42	$10.00	_____
17.		$12.75	$15.00	_____
18.		$13.51	$15.00	_____
19.		$19.72	$20.00	_____
20.		$3.83	$20.00	_____

Figure out how much money you will get in change.
Write your answers in the blanks using words.

21. Eighty-nine cents out of one dollar.   _eleven cents_

22. Forty-eight cents out of fifty cents.   _____

23. Sixty-four cents out of one dollar.   _____

24. Fifty cents out of one dollar.   _____

25. Seventy-eight cents out of eighty-five cents.   _____

26. Thirty-three cents out of one dollar.   _____

27. Sixty-five cents out of seventy-five cents.   _____

28. Thirty cents out of fifty cents.   _____

29. Thirty-one cents out of fifty cents.   _____

30. Six cents out of fifty cents.   _____

31. Twenty-four cents out of twenty-five cents.   _____

32. Eight cents out of twenty-five cents.   _____

33. Forty-three cents out of fifty cents.   _____

34. Seventeen cents out of fifty cents.   _____

35. Three cents out of ten cents.   _____

36. Three cents out of twenty-five cents.   _____

37. Three cents out of fifty cents   _____

38. Thirteen cents out of fifty cents.   _____

39. Thirty-six cents out of fifty cents.   _____

40. Nine cents out of twenty-five cents.   _____

41. Fourteen cents out of twenty-five cents.   _____

42. Four dollars out of five dollars.   _____

43. Forty-nine cents out of one dollar.   _____

44. Six dollars out of ten dollars.   _____

45. Twenty-seven cents out of fifty cents.   _____

Choosing Change

Draw a line from each problem to its correct change.

1. $ .37 out of $ .50 $ .03

   $ .55 out of $ .60 $ .07

   $ .63 out of $ .70 $ .17

   $ .58 out of $ .75 $ .05

   $ .67 out of $ .70 $ .13

2. $ .23 out of $ .50 $ .27

   $ .94 out of $1.00 $ .31

   $ .68 out of $ .75 $ .03

   $ .72 out of $ .75 $ .06

   $ .19 out of $ .50 $ .07

3. $1.85 out of $2.00 $ .85

   $1.76 out of $2.00 $ .10

   $1.15 out of $1.25 $ .15

   $1.15 out of $2.00 $ .54

   $1.46 out of $2.00 $ .24

4. $2.55 out of $2.75 $ .03

   $3.67 out of $3.70 $3.23

   $1.77 out of $5.00 $1.09

   $2.91 out of $4.00 $ .20

   $2.22 out of $2.30 $ .08

5. $ .98 out of $5.00 $ .49

   $3.16 out of $5.00 $ .89

   $ .88 out of $ .95 $4.02

   $1.01 out of $1.50 $1.84

   $ .11 out of $1.00 $ .07

6. $6.28 out of $6.50 $ .07

   $7.44 out of $7.50 $ .06

   $ .83 out of $5.00 $ .12

   $1.53 out of $1.60 $ .22

   $1.38 out of $1.50 $4.17

7. $9.34 out of $9.50 $3.04

   $6.96 out of $10.00 $ .06

   $1.20 out of $10.00 $8.80

   $2.80 out of $5.00 $ .16

   $ .64 out of $ .70 $2.20

8. $1.92 out of $2.00 $ .18

   $2.49 out of $5.00 $ .82

   $3.18 out of $4.00 $5.92

   $ .63 out of $5.00 $ .08

   $1.32 out of $1.50 $2.51

   $4.08 out of $10.00 $4.37

9. $5.25 out of $6.00 $1.50

   $2.75 out of $3.00 $ .25

   $5.00 out of $10.00 $ .50

   $3.50 out of $4.00 $ .75

   $10.00 out of $20.00 $5.00

   $8.50 out of $10.00 $10.00

10. $11.06 out of $12.00 $ .44

   $9.68 out of $20.00 $1.71

   $4.69 out of $20.00 $3.52

   $1.06 out of $1.50 $10.32

   $3.29 out of $5.00 $ .94

   $6.48 out of $10.00 $15.31

NAME _____

Find the answers to these subtraction problems.

1.	$ .29 − .07 $ .22	2.	$ .54 − .02	3.	$ .63 − .52	4.	$ .16 − .06	5.	$ .57 − .24
6.	$ .75 − .58	7.	$ .35 − .29	8.	$ .80 − .71	9.	$ .25 − .19	10.	$ .50 − .36
11.	$1.73 − .26 $1.47	12.	$1.82 − .72	13.	$2.87 − .24	14.	$2.32 −1.14	15.	$3.62 −1.18
16.	$4.50 −1.19	17.	$4.77 −3.18	18.	$6.28 −3.05	19.	$8.98 −5.43	20.	$9.41 −1.23
21.	$7.50 − .99	22.	$8.00 −3.67	23.	$5.00 −4.71	24.	$10.00 − 4.39	25.	$10.00 − 7.87
26.	$10.00 − 9.25	27.	$15.00 −12.66	28.	$14.75 −11.76	29.	$20.00 −17.43	30.	$20.00 − 2.79

Find the answers to these subtraction problems.

1. $10.00
   − .75
   $ 9.25

2. $10.00
   − .68

3. $10.00
   − .26

4. $10.00
   − .14

5. $10.50
   − 1.36

6. $22.75
   −12.52

7. $23.25
   −13.08

8. $24.50
   −14.41

9. $25.00
   −21.24

10. $25.00
    −23.49

11. $25.00
    − 7.56

12. $35.00
    − 2.38

13. $30.00
    −23.00

14. $40.00
    −12.50

15. $50.00
    −29.89

16. $50.00
    − 6.06

17. $45.00
    −10.50

18. $60.00
    − 8.17

19. $80.00
    −14.00

20. $90.00
    −45.45

21. 104
    − 94
    10

22. 476
    − 25

23. 186
    − 4

24. 319
    − 68

25. 588
    −173

26. 408
    −255

27. 711
    −614

28. 929
    −312

29. 200
    −133

30. 613
    −586

31. 1004
    −500

32. 1641
    −216

33. 2366
    −155

34. 3117
    −2002

35. 7069
    −2334

Cash Register Receipts

When you shop in a store, you usually buy more than one item at a time. The store clerk scans each item and the price is added on a cash register. The clerk then gives you a receipt. A cash register receipt shows how much each item costs. And it shows the total amount of money the items cost altogether. Some cash register receipts also show how much money the customer gives the clerk and how much the clerk gives in change.

Watch the cash register as the clerk adds up your purchases. Be sure the clerk gives you the correct change, too. Anyone can make a mistake. The clerk will be glad to have your help.

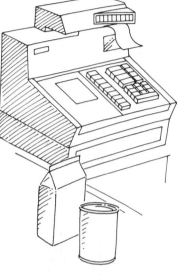

Finish these cash register receipts by adding up the cost of each item and filling in the totals. Then figure out your correct change by subtracting the totals from the amounts paid. Write in the correct change.

1.

$ .16	ITEM
.24	ITEM
.32	ITEM
.17	ITEM
$ .89	TOTAL
$1.00	PAID
$ .11	CHANGE

2.

$ .27	ITEM
.34	ITEM
.65	ITEM
.17	ITEM
	TOTAL
$1.50	PAID
	CHANGE

3.

$ .24	ITEM
.51	ITEM
.32	ITEM
.47	ITEM
	TOTAL
$2.00	PAID
	CHANGE

4.

$ .37	ITEM
.42	ITEM
.61	ITEM
.17	ITEM
.42	ITEM
	TOTAL
$2.00	PAID
	CHANGE

5.

$1.19	ITEM
1.12	ITEM
1.12	ITEM
.89	ITEM
.36	ITEM
	TOTAL
$5.00	PAID
	CHANGE

6.

$ .36	ITEM
.68	ITEM
1.21	ITEM
1.43	ITEM
1.05	ITEM
	TOTAL
$5.00	PAID
	CHANGE

7.

$ .47	ITEM
.41	ITEM
.62	ITEM
.35	ITEM
.61	ITEM
.74	ITEM
	TOTAL
$5.00	PAID
	CHANGE

8.

$1.14	ITEM
2.16	ITEM
.22	ITEM
.35	ITEM
2.17	ITEM
1.18	ITEM
	TOTAL
$8.00	PAID
	CHANGE

9.

$ .34	ITEM
.18	ITEM
.65	ITEM
2.52	ITEM
.22	ITEM
.22	ITEM
	TOTAL
$5.00	PAID
	CHANGE

10.

$1.14	ITEM
1.64	ITEM
.35	ITEM
2.15	ITEM
1.05	ITEM
1.19	ITEM
1.19	ITEM
	TOTAL
$9.00	PAID
	CHANGE

11.

$ .35	ITEM
.64	ITEM
1.71	ITEM
1.08	ITEM
1.08	ITEM
.38	ITEM
3.75	ITEM
	TOTAL
$10.00	PAID
	CHANGE

12.

$ 2.13	ITEM
1.89	ITEM
1.12	ITEM
1.12	ITEM
1.12	ITEM
10.75	ITEM
.54	ITEM
	TOTAL
$20.00	PAID
	CHANGE

13.

$11.24	ITEM
1.16	ITEM
.89	ITEM
.74	ITEM
.56	ITEM
3.10	ITEM
1.31	ITEM
.42	ITEM
	TOTAL
$20.00	PAID
	CHANGE

14.

$ 2.14	ITEM
2.14	ITEM
2.14	ITEM
1.33	ITEM
1.28	ITEM
.59	ITEM
.98	ITEM
11.05	ITEM
	TOTAL
$25.00	PAID
	CHANGE

15.

$ 3.62	ITEM
1.09	ITEM
1.15	ITEM
2.48	ITEM
.67	ITEM
4.00	ITEM
10.34	ITEM
10.34	ITEM
	TOTAL
$40.00	PAID
	CHANGE

Supermarket Maze

Start at the top left square of the maze. Follow the openings through the squares, adding the cost of each item as you go. (Do your work on another piece of paper.) Fill in the blanks for totals and change. Then answer the questions at the bottom of the page.

Enter here with $30.00 to spend.

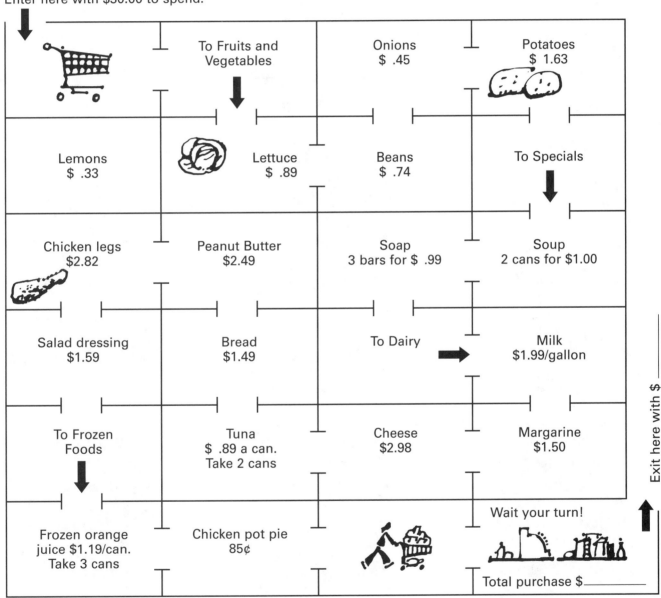

How much money did you spend in the supermarket altogether? _____

If you bought everything in the maze, how much would you spend? _____

Finish these cash register receipts by filling in the blanks.

1.
$ .37	ITEM
1.15	ITEM
.65	ITEM
.48	ITEM
2.11	ITEM
1.27	ITEM
$6.03	TOTAL
$7.00	PAID
$ .97	CHANGE

2.
$ 2.88	ITEM
.22	ITEM
1.18	ITEM
.81	ITEM
1.10	ITEM
.29	ITEM
	TOTAL
$10.00	PAID
	CHANGE

3.
$ .18	ITEM
2.11	ITEM
2.11	ITEM
2.11	ITEM
2.11	ITEM
.32	ITEM
	TOTAL
$10.00	PAID
	CHANGE

4.
$ 1.23	ITEM
2.19	ITEM
1.64	ITEM
.69	ITEM
1.09	ITEM
3.20	ITEM
.46	ITEM
	TOTAL
$20.00	PAID
	CHANGE

5.
$ .92	ITEM
3.14	ITEM
1.89	ITEM
.45	ITEM
.78	ITEM
4.35	ITEM
1.52	ITEM
	TOTAL
$20.00	PAID
	CHANGE

6.
$ 3.00	ITEM
1.25	ITEM
.98	ITEM
5.13	ITEM
1.49	ITEM
2.63	ITEM
.26	ITEM
	TOTAL
$20.00	PAID
	CHANGE

7.
$ 6.58	ITEM
1.24	ITEM
2.79	ITEM
.69	ITEM
3.07	ITEM
.99	ITEM
4.35	ITEM
	TOTAL
$20.00	PAID
	CHANGE

8.
$ 4.09	ITEM
.38	ITEM
2.88	ITEM
3.17	ITEM
5.97	ITEM
5.98	ITEM
1.14	ITEM
	TOTAL
$25.00	PAID
	CHANGE

9.
$10.00	ITEM
1.45	ITEM
3.04	ITEM
.89	ITEM
5.50	ITEM
4.48	ITEM
1.25	ITEM
	TOTAL
$30.00	PAID
	CHANGE

Find the mistakes in these receipts. Some show wrong totals, and some show the wrong change. Make your corrections on the lines next to each receipt.

1.

$ .84	ITEM
.59	ITEM
.76	ITEM
.23	ITEM
.09	ITEM
$2.51	TOTAL
$5.00	PAID
$2.39	CHANGE

_____ $2.49

2.

$ 4.20	ITEM
6.87	ITEM
9.32	ITEM
7.66	ITEM
3.85	ITEM
$31.90	TOTAL
$35.00	PAID
$3.20	CHANGE

_____

3.

$15.26	ITEM
6.21	ITEM
.89	ITEM
.89	ITEM
6.47	ITEM
$28.72	TOTAL
$30.00	PAID
$ .28	CHANGE

_____

4.

$ 2.34	ITEM
5.87	ITEM
6.11	ITEM
3.04	ITEM
2.58	ITEM
8.96	ITEM
$28.90	TOTAL
$30.00	PAID
$ 1.90	CHANGE

_____

5.

$13.79	ITEM
18.24	ITEM
12.66	ITEM
18.53	ITEM
17.22	ITEM
11.30	ITEM
$90.74	TOTAL
$95.00	PAID
$ 3.26	CHANGE

_____

6.

$ 7.84	ITEM
1.23	ITEM
25.46	ITEM
16.80	ITEM
14.07	ITEM
9.92	ITEM
$76.32	TOTAL
$80.00	PAID
$ 4.86	CHANGE

_____

7.

$ 5.33	ITEM
7.59	ITEM
12.50	ITEM
46.02	ITEM
3.29	ITEM
17.55	ITEM
$92.29	TOTAL
$95.00	PAID
$ 2.72	CHANGE

_____

8.

$ 5.27	ITEM
14.95	ITEM
17.20	ITEM
8.07	ITEM
3.79	ITEM
11.88	ITEM
$61.16	TOTAL
$70.00	PAID
$ 9.84	CHANGE

_____

9.

$15.08	ITEM
27.39	ITEM
8.17	ITEM
27.48	ITEM
6.33	ITEM
2.54	ITEM
$86.99	TOTAL
$90.00	PAID
$ 3.11	CHANGE

_____

10.

$ 7.77	ITEM
3.21	ITEM
8.59	ITEM
6.04	ITEM
8.31	ITEM
$32.92	TOTAL
$40.00	PAID
$ 6.08	CHANGE

$33.92 _____

11.

$ 9.20	ITEM
.79	ITEM
.79	ITEM
4.87	ITEM
2.29	ITEM
$27.94	TOTAL
$20.00	PAID
$2.06	CHANGE

_____

12.

$18.42	ITEM
25.56	ITEM
7.75	ITEM
4.10	ITEM
11.33	ITEM
$67.05	TOTAL
$70.00	PAID
$ 2.84	CHANGE

_____

13.

$ 1.59	ITEM
15.59	ITEM
6.28	ITEM
34.71	ITEM
22.06	ITEM
3.68	ITEM
$83.91	TOTAL
$90.00	PAID
$ 6.19	CHANGE

_____

14.

$15.48	ITEM
13.22	ITEM
14.98	ITEM
14.72	ITEM
12.85	ITEM
12.85	ITEM
$84.20	TOTAL
$90.00	PAID
$ 5.90	CHANGE

_____

15.

$ 5.69	ITEM
18.25	ITEM
7.83	ITEM
11.47	ITEM
1.49	ITEM
16.87	ITEM
$61.60	TOTAL
$70.00	PAID
$ 9.40	CHANGE

_____

16.

$ 1.25	ITEM
12.12	ITEM
6.06	ITEM
5.14	ITEM
17.19	ITEM
2.24	ITEM
1.18	ITEM
$44.18	TOTAL
$50.00	PAID
$ 4.82	CHANGE

_____

17.

$ 8.45	ITEM
4.44	ITEM
7.30	ITEM
.79	ITEM
13.65	ITEM
2.87	ITEM
1.76	ITEM
$39.26	TOTAL
$50.00	PAID
$11.73	CHANGE

_____

18.

$28.94	ITEM
12.35	ITEM
11.11	ITEM
7.82	ITEM
3.62	ITEM
15.49	ITEM
4.41	ITEM
$83.74	TOTAL
$85.00	PAID
$ 1.37	CHANGE

_____

Buying More Than One of the Same Item

Sometimes you will buy more than one of the same item when you shop. Suppose you are buying four cans of the same soup. The soup costs eighty-two cents a can.

82¢   82¢   82¢   82¢

You can find the total cost of the soup two different ways. You can add the price of each can.

$ .82   price 1 can
  .82   price 1 can
  .82   price 1 can
+ .82   price 1 can
$3.28   Total Cost

Or you can use a shortcut. You can *multiply* the price of a single can by the number of cans you are buying.

$ .82   price 1 can
×   4   number of cans
$3.28   Total Cost

Remember, you can only use this *multiplication* shortcut when the items you buy have exactly the same price. You would read the example above as, "Four times eighty-two cents equals three dollars and twenty-eight cents."

Here is another example. You are buying 3 pounds of meat at three dollars and twenty-three cents a pound.

Adding
$3.23   price 1 pound
  3.23   price 1 pound
+3.23   price 1 pound
$9.69   Total Cost

Multiplying
$3.23   price 1 pound
×   3   number of pounds
$9.69   Total Cost

These examples show you how much easier it is to use multiplication than addition to find your total cost when you are buying more than one of the same item.

In these exercises, you are buying more than one of the same item in a grocery store. Find the total cost of each purchase by adding the price of each item. Then write the multiplication problem that also shows you the total cost of that item.

1.

```
$  .79
   .79
   .79
   .79
+  .79
_____
```

$\begin{array}{r} \$ \ . \ 7 \ 9 \\ \times \qquad 5 \\ \hline \_\_ . \_\_ \_\_ \end{array}$ **Total Cost**

2.

```
$  .83
   .83
   .83
   .83
   .83
+  .83
_____
```

$\begin{array}{r} \$ \ . \_\_ \_\_ \\ \times \qquad \_\_ \\ \hline \_\_ . \_\_ \_\_ \end{array}$ **Total Cost**

3.

```
$  .92
   .92
   .92
+  .92
_____
```

$\begin{array}{r} \$ \ . \_\_ \_\_ \\ \times \qquad \_\_ \\ \hline \_\_ . \_\_ \_\_ \end{array}$ **Total Cost**

4.

```
$ 1.99
  1.99
  1.99
  1.99
  1.99
  1.99
  1.99
  1.99
  1.99
  1.99
  1.99
+ 1.99
_____
```

$\begin{array}{r} 1 \ . \ 9 \ 9 \\ \times \qquad \\ \hline 3 \ 9 \ 8 \\ + \ 1 \ 9 \ 9 \ 0 \\ \hline \$ \ 2 \ 3 \ . \ 8 \ 8 \end{array}$ **Total Cost**

NAME _____

In these exercises, you are buying more than one of the same item in a grocery store. Use multiplication to find the total cost for each purchase. Then write this amount in the blank. (Show your multiplication work in the space next to the pictures.)

1. 4 cans of tomatoes = $ ___3.16___

$$\begin{array}{r} \$ \ .79 \\ \times \quad 4 \\ \hline \$3.16 \end{array}$$

79¢ a can

2. 3 cans of beans = $ _____

65¢ a can

3. 3 heads of lettuce = $ _____

89¢ a head

4. 2 loaves of bread = $ _____

$1.29 a loaf

5. 2 quarts of milk = $ _____

74¢ a quart

6. 6 boxes of raisins = $ _____

$1.15 a box

7. 8 cucumbers = $ _____

38¢ each

8. 3 pounds of carrots = $ _____

39¢ a pound

9. 5 lemons = $ _____

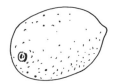

29¢ each

10. 2 boxes of cake mix = $ _____

99¢ each

11. 7 ears of corn = $ _____

23¢ an ear

12. 6 grapefruits = $ _____

52¢ each

13. 4 cans of peas = $ _____

65¢ a can

14. 3 pounds of cheese = $ _____

$3.59 a pound

15. 3 pineapples = $ _____

$1.25 each

16. 5 pounds of apples = $ _____

69¢ a pound

17. 2 jars of honey = $ _____

$2.95 each

18. 4-pound chicken = $ _____

89¢ a pound

19. 4 pounds of bananas = $ _____

34¢ a pound

20. 3 boxes of crackers = $ _____

$1.12 each

In these exercises, you are buying more than one of the same item in a grocery store. Use multiplication to find the total cost for each purchase. Then write this amount in the blank. (Show your multiplication work in the space next to the pictures.)

1. 12-pound turkey = $ ___8.28___

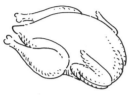

```
$ .69
X  12
  138
  69
$8.28
```

69¢ a pound

2. 12 cans of soup = $ _____

82¢ a can

3. 12 cans of soft drink = $ _____

39¢ a can

4. 8-pound ham = $ _____

$2.25 a pound

5. 6-pound roast = $ _____

$2.28 a pound

6. 14-pound watermelon = $ _____

17¢ a pound

7. 4 gallons of milk = $ _____

$1.99 a gallon

8. 10 pounds of potatoes = $ _____

27¢ a pound

9. 25 pounds of dog food = $ _____

42¢ a pound

10. 10 pounds of sugar = $ _____

48¢ a pound

11. 5 pounds of flour = $ _____

32¢ a pound

12. 5 pounds of fish = $ _____

$3.49 a pound

13. 15 pounds of ice = $ _____

14¢ a pound

14. 4 pounds of coffee = $ _____

$2.21 a pound

15. 12 pounds of apples = $ _____

59¢ a pound

16. 14 pounds of peaches = $ _____

79¢ a pound

17. 16-pound pumpkin = $ _____

12¢ a pound

18. 11 pounds of onions = $ _____

36¢ a pound

19. 3 cans of nuts = $ _____

$4.19 a can

20. 12 cans of juice = $ _____

79¢ a can

NAME _____

Find the answers to these multiplication problems.

1.   9¢
  × 3
  27¢

2.   2¢
  × 5

3.   8¢
  × 2

4.   6¢
  × 4

5.   4¢
  × 9

6. $ .10
  × 8
  $ .80

7. $ .14
  × 7

8. $ .20
  × 5

9. $ .23
  × 6

10. $ .09
  × 9

11. $ .96
  × 7

12. $ .84
  × 5

13. $ .72
  × 7

14. $ .37
  × 8

15. $ .54
  × 6

16. $1.25
  × 3

17. $1.04
  × 5

18. $1.89
  × 2

19. $2.50
  × 9

20. $2.62
  × 6

21. $5.50
  × 10
  $55.00

22. $6.33
  × 12

23. $1.12
  × 18

24. $8.46
  × 11

25. $ .87
  × 20

26. $3.37
  × 26
  2022
  6740
  $87.62

27. $2.46
  × 13

28. $3.94
  × 25

29. $1.83
  × 50

30. $4.65
  × 19

Find the answers to these multiplication problems.

1. $\begin{array}{r} 7 \\ \times\ 7 \\ \hline 49 \end{array}$
2. $\begin{array}{r} 9 \\ \times\ 5 \\ \hline \end{array}$
3. $\begin{array}{r} 8 \\ \times\ 4 \\ \hline \end{array}$
4. $\begin{array}{r} 4 \\ \times\ 8 \\ \hline \end{array}$
5. $\begin{array}{r} 6 \\ \times\ 9 \\ \hline \end{array}$

6. $\begin{array}{r} 23 \\ \times\ 4 \\ \hline 92 \end{array}$
7. $\begin{array}{r} 47 \\ \times\ 5 \\ \hline \end{array}$
8. $\begin{array}{r} 84 \\ \times\ 7 \\ \hline \end{array}$
9. $\begin{array}{r} 97 \\ \times\ 9 \\ \hline \end{array}$
10. $\begin{array}{r} 57 \\ \times\ 2 \\ \hline \end{array}$

11. $\begin{array}{r} 49 \\ \times\ 8 \\ \hline \end{array}$
12. $\begin{array}{r} 36 \\ \times\ 4 \\ \hline \end{array}$
13. $\begin{array}{r} 24 \\ \times\ 6 \\ \hline \end{array}$
14. $\begin{array}{r} 43 \\ \times\ 9 \\ \hline \end{array}$
15. $\begin{array}{r} 68 \\ \times\ 8 \\ \hline \end{array}$

16. $\begin{array}{r} 111 \\ \times\ 7 \\ \hline \end{array}$
17. $\begin{array}{r} 234 \\ \times\ 9 \\ \hline \end{array}$
18. $\begin{array}{r} 569 \\ \times\ 3 \\ \hline \end{array}$
19. $\begin{array}{r} 352 \\ \times\ 4 \\ \hline \end{array}$
20. $\begin{array}{r} 718 \\ \times\ 5 \\ \hline \end{array}$

21. $\begin{array}{r} 405 \\ \times\ 10 \\ \hline 4{,}050 \end{array}$
22. $\begin{array}{r} 51 \\ \times\ 13 \\ \hline \end{array}$
23. $\begin{array}{r} 128 \\ \times\ 34 \\ \hline \end{array}$
24. $\begin{array}{r} 346 \\ \times\ 27 \\ \hline \end{array}$
25. $\begin{array}{r} 293 \\ \times\ 33 \\ \hline \end{array}$

26. $\begin{array}{r} 376 \\ \times\ 24 \\ \hline 1504 \\ 7520 \\ \hline 9{,}024 \end{array}$
27. $\begin{array}{r} 146 \\ \times\ 53 \\ \hline \end{array}$
28. $\begin{array}{r} 492 \\ \times\ 16 \\ \hline \end{array}$
29. $\begin{array}{r} 314 \\ \times\ 29 \\ \hline \end{array}$
30. $\begin{array}{r} 278 \\ \times\ 27 \\ \hline \end{array}$

What Will It Cost?

Find the total cost of each of the grocery orders below.
Do your work on another piece of paper.

 99¢

 Lemons 29¢ each

 34¢ lb.

 89¢

 39¢ lb.

 23¢

 Cucumbers 38¢ each

1. 4 lemons $ __1.16__
    2 heads of lettuce $ __1.78__
           Total $ __2.94__

2. 3 bags of nuts $ _____
    5 pounds of bananas $ _____
           Total $ _____

3. 6 cucumbers $ _____
    3 pounds of carrots $ _____
    2 lemons $ _____
           Total $ _____

4. 8 ears of corn $ _____
    3 cucumbers $ _____
    4 heads of lettuce $ _____
           Total $ _____

5. 5 cucumbers $ _____
    3 heads of lettuce $ _____
    4 ears of corn $ _____
           Total $ _____

6. 5 bags of nuts $ _____
    7 pounds of bananas $ _____
    8 cucumbers $ _____
           Total $ _____

7. 3 lemons $ _____
    6 cucumbers $ _____
    7 pounds of carrots $ _____
           Total $ _____

8. 12 ears of corn $ _____
    3 pounds of bananas $ _____
    5 heads of lettuce $ _____
           Total $ _____

 $2.95
 $1.29
 $1.80
 $3.92

 $2.98
 Grapefruit 52¢ each
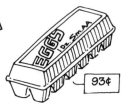 93¢
 Ham $2.25 lb.
 $4.89

9. 3 grapefruits $ _1.56_
     2 boxes of cereal $ _5.96_
           Total $ _7.52_

10. 2 jars of jam $ _____
      3 loaves of bread $ _____
           Total $ _____

11. 2 dozen eggs $ _____
      2 pounds of ham $ _____
      4 loaves of bread $ _____
           Total $ _____

12. 3 jars of honey $ _____
      2 gallons of juice $ _____
      2 cans of coffee $ _____
           Total $ _____

13. 3 jars of jam $ _____
      4 boxes of cereal $ _____
      6 grapefruits $ _____
           Total $ _____

14. 3 dozen eggs $ _____
      2 jars of honey $ _____
      3 gallons of juice $ _____
           Total $ _____

15. 5 pounds of ham $ _____
      2 loaves of bread $ _____
      3 cans of coffee $ _____
           Total $ _____

16. 4 jars of jam $ _____
      3 boxes of cereal $ _____
      4 grapefruits $ _____
           Total $ _____

NAME _____

Find the total cost of each of these department store orders. Do your work on another piece of paper.

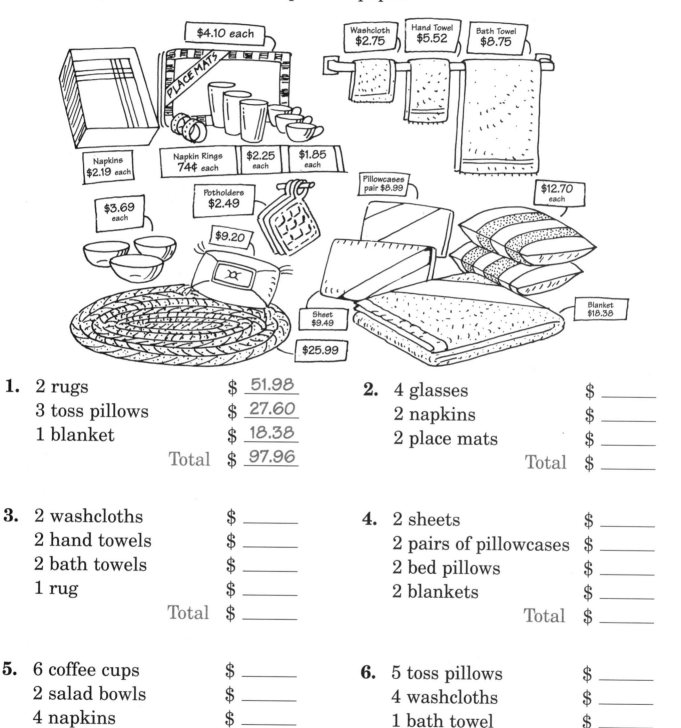

1. 2 rugs $ <u>51.98</u>
3 toss pillows $ <u>27.60</u>
1 blanket $ <u>18.38</u>
          Total $ <u>97.96</u>

2. 4 glasses $ _____
2 napkins $ _____
2 place mats $ _____
       Total $ _____

3. 2 washcloths $ _____
2 hand towels $ _____
2 bath towels $ _____
1 rug $ _____
       Total $ _____

4. 2 sheets $ _____
2 pairs of pillowcases $ _____
2 bed pillows $ _____
2 blankets $ _____
       Total $ _____

5. 6 coffee cups $ _____
2 salad bowls $ _____
4 napkins $ _____
4 napkin rings $ _____
3 pot holders $ _____
       Total $ _____

6. 5 toss pillows $ _____
4 washcloths $ _____
1 bath towel $ _____
2 place mats $ _____
1 sheet $ _____
       Total $ _____

7. 6 glasses $ _____
       4 coffee cups $ _____
       4 place mats $ _____
       4 salad bowls $ _____
       2 toss pillows $ _____
       1 hand towel $ _____
          Total $ _____

8. 3 sheets $ _____
       1 pair pillowcases $ _____
       1 bed pillow $ _____
       2 pot holders $ _____
       2 coffee cups $ _____
       3 washcloths $ _____
          Total $ _____

9. 6 napkins $ _____
       6 napkin rings $ _____
       6 place mats $ _____
          Total $ _____

10. 8 glasses $ _____
       3 salad bowls $ _____
       1 toss pillow $ _____
          Total $ _____

11. 4 bath towels $ _____
       3 pairs of pillowcases $ _____
       1 washcloth $ _____
       4 pot holders $ _____
          Total $ _____

12. 8 napkins $ _____
       8 place mats $ _____
       8 napkin rings $ _____
       6 pot holders $ _____
          Total $ _____

13. 3 bed pillows $ _____
       4 toss pillows $ _____
       6 salad bowls $ _____
          Total $ _____

14. 3 blankets $ _____
       2 glasses $ _____
       1 pot holder $ _____
          Total $ _____

15. 5 coffee cups $ _____
       5 hand towels $ _____
          Total $ _____

16. 3 bath towels $ _____
       4 sheets $ _____
          Total $ _____

17. 24 napkins $ _____
       24 napkin rings $ _____
          Total $ _____

18. 12 glasses $ _____
       14 place mats $ _____
          Total $ _____

NAME _____

Multiply the numbers and coins between the spokes of the wheel. Start at the center and work out to the rim of the wheel. Write the totals in the blanks along the rim.

For example: $5 \times 8 \times 2 \times \$ .36 =$ ___$28.80___

Total $28.80

Total _____

Total _____

Total _____

How much money is in the wheel altogether? _____
Add the totals around the rim of the wheel. What is the sum? _____

Multiply each line of numbers and coins from the center out. Write the totals in the answer boxes using the dollar sign and decimal point.

For example: $10 \times \$.01 \times 1 \times 5$ is $.50

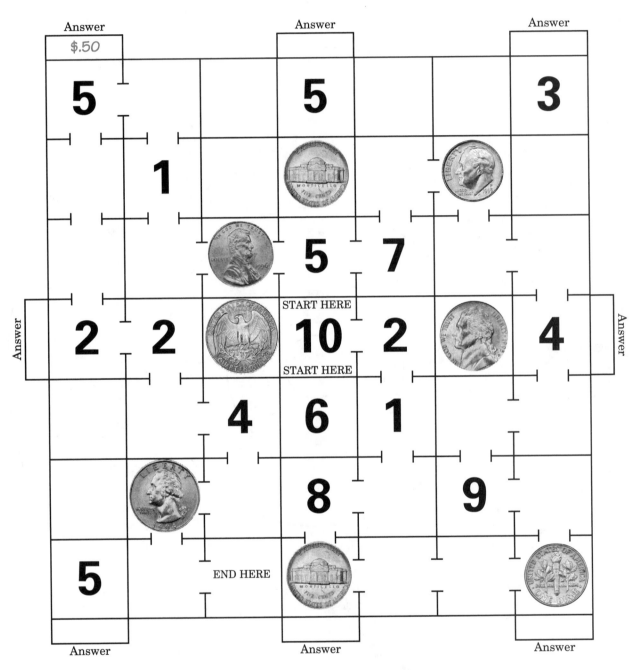

Now, to work the maze, start in the center and follow the openings. As you pass through each square, add the numbers and coins. Start with 10, add 2, add 1, add 8, add .05, and so on: $(10 + 2 + 1 + 8 + .05 \ldots)$.

Write your final total here: _____

NAME _____

GreenBeans
3 for 99¢

In stores you will often see signs that give the sale price for more than one of the same item. Suppose canned green beans are priced 3 for 99¢. You can find the cost of one can by using *division,* like this:

$$\frac{33¢}{3)\overline{99¢}} \text{ or } 99¢ \div 3 = 33¢$$ **The cost of one can of green beans is 33¢.**

You would read this: "Three goes into ninety-nine thirty-three times" or "Ninety-nine cents divided by three equals thirty-three cents."

Suppose a sign in a store says that canned tomatoes are 2 for $1.28. To find the cost of one can of tomatoes, divide:

Canned
Tomatoes
2 for $1.28

$$\frac{\$ .64}{2)\overline{\$1.28}} \text{ or } \$1.28 \div 2 = \$.64$$ **The cost of one can of tomatoes is $.64.**

You can use the Multiplication Table on page 127 to help you divide. To work division problems, you use the table in the opposite way you use it to work multiplication problems. For the first problem below, find the number of items (2) in the column at the left of the table. Read along the row until you find the first number you need to divide (19), or the closest number that is less than the first number you need to divide (18). Go to the top row of that column to get the answer to that part of your division problem (9). Now finish the problem. Find the cost for each item in the problems below. Write your answers in the blanks. (Show your division work next to each problem. If you need more room, use another piece of paper for your work. Label each problem.)

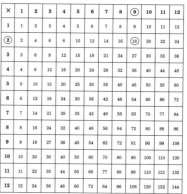

×	1	2	3	4	5	6	7	8	⑨	10	11	12
1	1	2	3	4	5	6	7	8	9	10	11	12
②	2	4	6	8	10	12	14	16	⑱	20	22	24
3	3	6	9	12	15	18	21	24	27	30	33	36
4	4	8	12	16	20	24	28	32	36	40	44	48
5	5	10	15	20	25	30	35	40	45	50	55	60
6	6	12	18	24	30	36	42	48	54	60	66	72
7	7	14	21	28	35	42	49	56	63	70	77	84
8	8	16	24	32	40	48	56	64	72	80	88	96
9	9	18	27	36	45	54	63	72	81	90	99	108
10	10	20	30	40	50	60	70	80	90	100	110	120
11	11	22	33	44	55	66	77	88	99	110	121	132
12	12	24	36	48	60	72	84	96	108	120	132	144

1.  for $1.98

number of items

total cost

$$\frac{\$ .99}{2)\overline{\$1.98}}$$
$$-18$$
$$18$$
$$-18$$
$$0$$

1 costs ___$.99___

2. for $2.72

$$\frac{\$.}{4)\overline{\$2.72}}$$

1 costs _____

3. 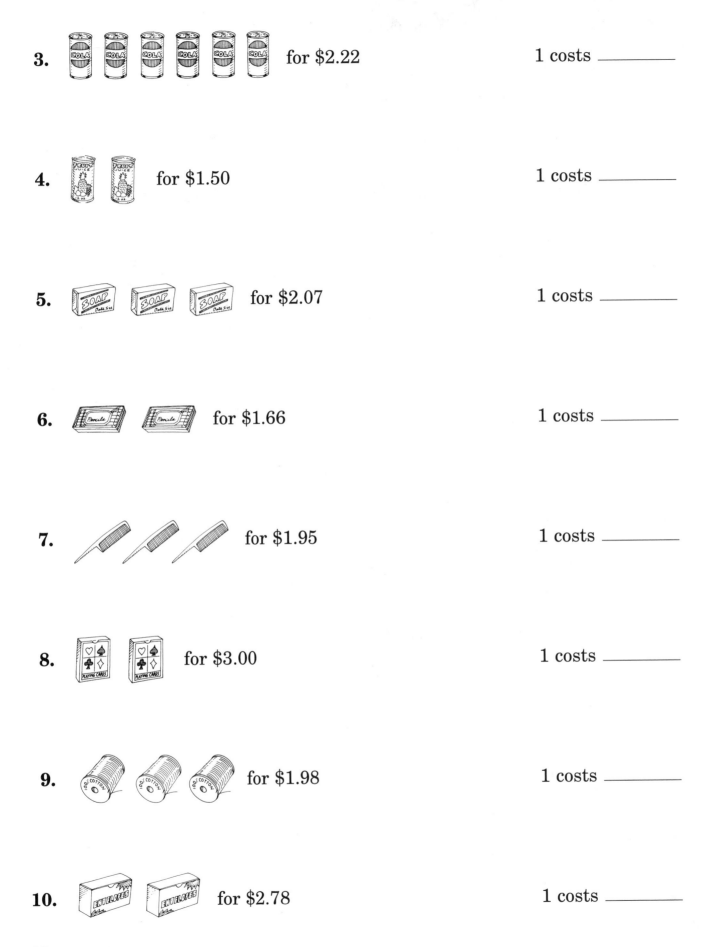 for $2.22   1 costs _____

4. for $1.50   1 costs _____

5. for $2.07   1 costs _____

6. for $1.66   1 costs _____

7. for $1.95   1 costs _____

8. for $3.00   1 costs _____

9. for $1.98   1 costs _____

10. for $2.78   1 costs _____

NAME _____

Use division to find the cost for one of each item on sale in these problems. Write your answers in the blanks. (Show your division work next to each problem. If you need more room, use another piece of paper for your work. Label each problem.)

1.  for $2.98

$$\begin{array}{r} \$1.49 \\ 2)\overline{\$2.98} \\ -2 \\ \hline 09 \\ -8 \\ \hline 18 \\ -18 \\ \hline 0 \end{array}$$

1 costs ___$1.49___

2. for $1.92

1 costs _____

3. 3 for $5.07

1 costs _____

4.  for $6.36

1 costs _____

5. 6 for $4.38

1 costs _____

6. for $3.30

1 costs _____

7. 9 for $3.87

1 costs _____

8. 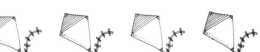 for $9.96

1 costs _____

9. 5 for $3.00

1 costs _____

10. for $2.58

1 costs _____

11. 8 for $5.52

1 costs _____

12. for $5.16

1 costs _____

	Item	Price		One Costs
13.		12 for $3.96	$\begin{array}{r} \$.33 \\ 12)\overline{\$3.96} \\ -3\,6 \\ \hline 36 \\ -36 \\ \hline 0 \end{array}$	$\underline{\$\ .33}$
14.		12 for $3.48		_____
15.		10 lb. for $6.70		_____
16.		11 lb. for $1.21		_____
17.		6 for $6.96		_____
18.		2 for $24.00		_____
19.		3 pairs for $3.75		_____
20.		5 rolls for $10.35		_____
21.		12 cards for $6.00		_____
22.		10 lb. for $1.70		_____

Finding the Price per Unit

Stores often carry different sizes, brands, or forms of the same item. The size of the product will appear on the label in units such as ounces, pounds, pints, or quarts. To find the best deal, you need to know the price per unit. There is a table showing the different units on page 128.

Suppose a 9-ounce box of cereal costs $2.34. A 12-ounce box of the same cereal costs $2.88. Which size should you buy to get the lowest price? You can find out how much each box of cereal costs per ounce by using division, like this:

```
          $ .26   per ounce.
9 oz.   )$2.34
         -1 8
           54
          -54
            0
```
The 9-ounce box of cereal costs $.26 per ounce.

```
          $ .24   per ounce.
12 oz.  )$2.88
         -2 4
           48
          -48
            0
```
The 12-ounce box of cereal costs $.24 per ounce.

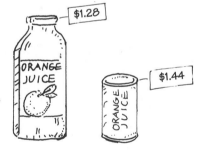

Now suppose a 32-ounce bottle of orange juice costs $1.28. A can of frozen orange juice makes 48 ounces of juice when mixed with water. The can costs $1.44. Which size costs less per ounce?

```
          $ .04
32 oz.  )$1.28
         -1 28
             0
```
The 32-ounce bottle costs $.04 per ounce of juice.

```
          $ .03
48 oz.  )$1.44
         -1 44
             0
```
The 48 ounces costs $.03 per ounce of juice.

Find the price per unit for each item in the problems below. (Show your division work next to each problem. If you need more room, use another piece of paper for your work. Label each problem.) Write your answers in the blanks.

1. $2.24 $3.08

7 oz.   11 oz.

$$\begin{array}{r} \$\ .32 \\ 7oz.\overline{)\$2.24} \\ -21 \\ \hline 14 \\ -14 \\ \hline 0 \end{array} \qquad \begin{array}{r} \$\ .28 \\ 11oz.\overline{)\$3.08} \\ -22 \\ \hline 88 \\ -88 \\ \hline 0 \end{array}$$

7 ounces $ .32

11 ounces $ .28

2. $3.92 $2.18

4 qt.   2 qt.

4 quarts _____

2 quarts _____

3. $1.16 $1.86

4 oz.   6 oz.

4 ounces _____

6 ounces _____

4. $2.28 $1.68

12 oz.   8 oz.

12 ounces _____

8 ounces _____

5. $4.36 $7.28

4 oz.   7 oz.

4 ounces _____

7 ounces _____

6. $8.67 $11.25

3 lb.   5 lb.

3 pounds _____

5 pounds _____

Finding the Price per Unit

Some stores make it easy to compare prices of different-sized items. You can find small signs on the front of the shelves, under the items. The signs list the price per unit.

These signs show that tuna costs less if you buy it in the bigger can. The tuna costs 16 cents an ounce in the six-ounce can, but only 13 cents in the ten-ounce can.

1. What is the cost per pound of dog food
   in the 25-pound bag? _____
   in the 10-pound bag? _____
   Which bag costs less per pound? _____

2. What is the cost per ounce of corn chips
   in the 11-ounce bag? _____
   in the 12-ounce bag? _____
   Which bag costs less per ounce? _____

3. What is the cost per pint of potato salad
   in the 16-ounce size? _____
   in the 8-ounce size? _____
   Which size costs less per pint? _____

Add up the money between each two spokes of the
wheel in the outer ring. Divide each total by the number
in the next ring. Write your answers in the inner ring.
For example, $1.50 divided by 10 is $ .15.

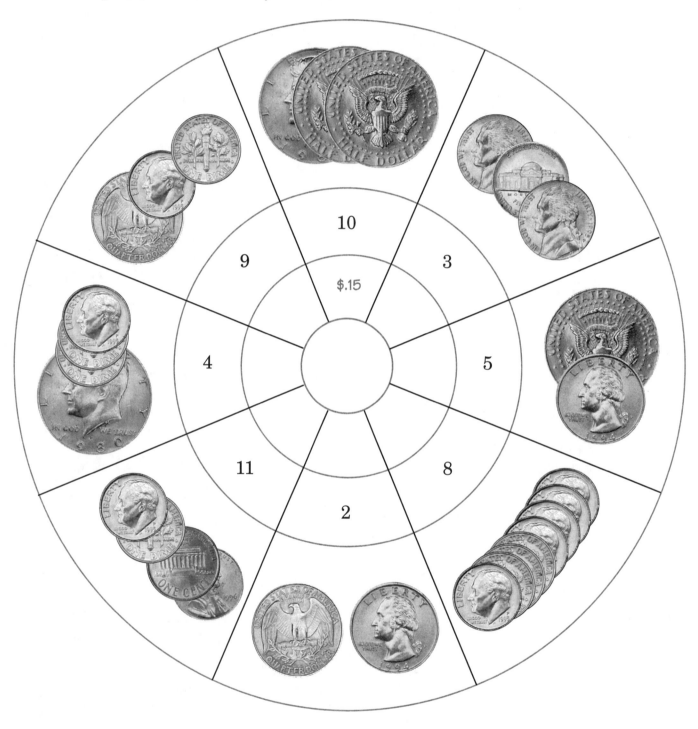

Add all the coins in the outer ring. What is the sum? _____

NAME _____

Find the answers to these division problems.

1.
$$\begin{array}{r} \$\ .15 \\ 3\overline{)\$\ .45} \\ -3 \\ \hline 15 \\ -15 \\ \hline 0 \end{array}$$

2. $5\overline{)\$\ .75}$

3. $7\overline{)\$\ .35}$

4. $6\overline{)\$\ .54}$

5. $8\overline{)\$\ .72}$

6. $4\overline{)\$\ .64}$

7. $2\overline{)\$2.36}$

8. $9\overline{)\$1.89}$

9.
$$\begin{array}{r} \$\ .37 \\ 5\overline{)\$1.85} \\ -15 \\ \hline 35 \\ -35 \\ \hline 0 \end{array}$$

10. $2\overline{)\$1.74}$

11. $8\overline{)\$1.92}$

12. $4\overline{)\$1.56}$

13. $3\overline{)\$13.35}$

14. $7\overline{)\$15.96}$

15. $9\overline{)\$12.87}$

16. $5\overline{)\$13.90}$

17. $6\overline{)\$16.32}$

18. $8\overline{)\$13.12}$

19. $10\overline{)\$3.90}$

20. $12\overline{)\$1.44}$

21. $24\overline{)\$4.80}$

22. $10\overline{)\$2.90}$

23. $15\overline{)\$3.45}$

24. $11\overline{)\$1.32}$

Find the answers to these division problems.

1.
$$\begin{array}{r} \$\ 9.76 \\ 2\overline{)\$19.52} \\ -18 \\ \hline 15 \\ -14 \\ \hline 12 \\ -12 \\ \hline 0 \end{array}$$

2. $9\overline{)\$30.60}$

3. $11\overline{)\$25.30}$

4. $4\overline{)\$15.04}$

5. $6\overline{)\$12.66}$

6. $8\overline{)\$32.16}$

7. $5\overline{)\$25.25}$

8. $7\overline{)\$21.14}$

9.
$$\begin{array}{r} 712 \\ 3\overline{)2136} \\ -21 \\ \hline 03 \\ -3 \\ \hline 06 \\ -6 \\ \hline 0 \end{array}$$

10. $2\overline{)1624}$

11. $9\overline{)1827}$

12. $10\overline{)4580}$

13. $7\overline{)4907}$

14. $8\overline{)5632}$

15. $12\overline{)3660}$

16. $6\overline{)6096}$

17. $3\overline{)9543}$

18. $5\overline{)8090}$

19. $4\overline{)2816}$

20. $2\overline{)5590}$

21. $12\overline{)4680}$

22. $11\overline{)6721}$

23. $24\overline{)2688}$

24. $14\overline{)1708}$

Saving Money at Sales

You can often save money by buying more than one of the same item when you shop. When an item is on special sale, you may save even more. Here is an example. Suppose the regular price for a baseball ticket is $8.50, but for one game you can buy two tickets for $15.50. (You must buy two to get the special price.)

What would be the regular price for two tickets?

$8.50	regular price of one
$\times$ 2	number of tickets
$17.00	regular price of two tickets

How much money would you save buying the two specially priced tickets?

$17.00	regular price of two tickets
$-15.50	special price of two tickets
$1.50	savings on two tickets

How much money would you save on each ticket?

$ .75	saving on each ticket
tickets 2)$1.50	saving on two tickets
-14	
10	
-10	
0	

Of course, you would have to decide whether or not you could *use* two tickets. A sale price is no bargain if you cannot use the quantity you have to buy.

Here is another example. Hanging plants are on sale at three for $18.99. The regular price is $6.79 each.

What would be the regular price for three plants?

$6.79
$\times$ 3
$20.37

How much would you save buying three plants on sale?

$20.37
-18.99
$1.38

How much would you save on each plant?

$ .46
3)$1.38

Find the total amount of money you would save in these sales. Then divide to find out how much you would save on each item. Do your work on another piece of paper. Write your answers in the blanks.

	Item	Regular Price	Sale Price	Total Saving	Saving Each Item
1.	RADISH SEEDS	59¢ each	2 for $1.00	$ .18	$ .09
2.	MILK 1GAL	$1.89 each	2 for $3.50		
3.	NOTE BOOK	$2.09 each	2 for $3.88		
4.	YARN	$1.69 each	5 for $6.25		
5.	TENNIS BALLS	$2.59 a can	3 for $6.87		
6.		$5.35 each	3 for $13.05		
7.		$1.38 each	4 for $3.92		
8.		29¢ each	7 for $1.33		
9.	SALTINES	$1.11 a box	2 for $1.78		
10.		$8.38 each	2 for $12.50		

Saving Money at Sales

Find the total amount of money you would save in these sales. Then divide to find out how much you would save on each item. Do your work on another piece of paper. Write your answers in the blanks.

	Item	Regular Price	Sale Price	Total Saving	Saving Each Item
1.		$4.49 each	2 for $6.00	$2.98	$1.49
2.		$3.42 each	3 for $8.97		
3.		$7.52 each	2 for $12.22		
4.		$5.79 a roll	4 for $18.00		
5.		$8.20 each	2 for $14.30		
6.		$5.62 a pair	2 pair for $8.66		
7.		$2.25 each	12 for $24.00		
8.		$21.95 each	2 for $33.90		

Here are two food store advertisements from a newspaper. Read them carefully. Figure out which store offers each item at the best price for the quantity you are buying. Then find out how much money this saves. Your answers go on the opposite page.

BLUE STAR SUPERMARKET
Nobody Beats Our Prices!

Ham—3-lb. can—$8.42

Eggs—89¢ a dozen

Corn—35¢ an ear

Tomatoes—79¢ lb.

Milk—½ gallon—92¢

Orange juice—6-oz. can—89¢

Potatoes—5-lb. bag—99¢

Cheese—sliced—16-oz. package—$2.79

Chicken—whole—69¢ lb.

Lunch meat—6-oz. package—$1.39

Bread—whole wheat—$1.19 a loaf

Bananas—3 lb. for 75¢

Peas—2 cans for $1.00

Celery—92¢ each

Yogurt—6-oz. cartons—3 for $1.95

Hamburger—extra lean—$2.49 lb.

Lettuce—2 heads for $1.70

Onions—5-lb. bag for $1.80

Strawberry jam—16-oz. jar—$1.98

Flour—5-lb. bag—$1.79

Joe's Market
LOWEST PRICES IN TOWN!

Ham—3-lb. can—$8.78

Eggs—93¢ a dozen

Corn—4 ears for $1.00

Tomatoes—3 lb. for $1.77

Milk—1 gallon—$1.99

Orange juice—12-oz. can—$1.29

Potatoes—10-lb. bag—$1.89

Cheese—sliced—8-oz. package—$1.69

Chicken—whole—85¢ lb.

Lunch meat—12-oz. package—$2.39

Bread—whole wheat—2 loaves for $1.98

Bananas—34¢ lb.

Peas—67¢ a can

Celery—2 for $1.82

Yogurt—6-oz. carton—82¢

Hamburger—extra lean—3 lb. for $6.00

Lettuce—85¢ a head

Onions—49¢ lb.

Strawberry jam—8-oz. jar—$1.19

Flour—10-lb. bag—$3.18

Item	Store with Lower Price	Buying	Money Saved
1. peas	Blue Star	6 cans	$1.02
2. lettuce	_____	2 heads	_____
3. flour	_____	10 lb.	_____
4. ham	_____	3-lb. can	_____
5. eggs	_____	1 dozen	_____
6. orange juice	_____	12 oz.	_____
7. cheese	_____	16 oz.	_____
8. celery	_____	two	_____
9. chicken	_____	6 lb.	_____
10. lunch meat	_____	24 oz.	_____
11. bread	_____	4 loaves	_____
12. corn	_____	10 ears	_____
13. hamburger	_____	3 lb.	_____
14. onions	_____	5 lb.	_____
15. bananas	_____	3 lb.	_____
16. yogurt	_____	6 cartons	_____
17. strawberry jam	_____	32 oz.	_____
18. potatoes	_____	10 lb.	_____
19. tomatoes	_____	6 lb.	_____
20. milk	_____	2 gallons	_____

How much money would you save if you bought everything at the lower price? _____

Here are four food store advertisements from a newspaper. Read them carefully and figure out which store offers each different item at the lowest unit price. Make a check mark in front of each of these best buys.

Boulevard Co-op

✔ Green Beans—2 cans for 70¢
Raisins—3-oz. boxes—4 for $1.49
Cereal—12-oz. box—$2.80
Soup—6 cans for $5.34
Apple juice—1 gallon—$3.92
Coffee—2-lb. can—$4.89
Butter—$1.79 lb.
Milk—69¢ a quart
Fresh fish—$3.49 lb.
Tomato juice—48-oz. can—$1.18
Crackers—$1.20 a box
Turkey—79¢ lb.
Mixed nuts—6-oz. can—$2.15
Sugar—5 lb. bag—$2.45

Larry's Market

Fresh fish—2 lb. for $6.00
Soft drinks—6 cans for $2.22
Cucumbers—4 for $1.00
Rolled roast—$2.79 lb.
Tomato juice—24-oz. can—74¢
Turkey—10 lb. for $7.50
Green beans—39¢ a can
Mixed nuts—12-oz. can—$4.18
Pineapples—$1.19 each
Raisins—12-oz. box—$1.28
Soup—3 cans for $1.50
Crackers—89¢ a box
Carrots—45¢ lb.
Apple juice—½ gallon—$1.99

Stone Supermarket

Butter—½ lb.—95¢
Carrots—39¢ lb.
Rolled roast—$2.96 lb.
Crackers—$1.05 a box
Milk—72¢ a quart
Cereal—12-oz. box—$2.68
Green beans—2 cans for 74¢
Cucumbers—36¢ each
Fresh fish—$3.29 lb.
Soup—79¢ a can
Coffee—$2.34 lb.
Tomato juice—24-oz. can—89¢
Pineapples—99¢ each
Soft drinks—12 cans for $4.20

Central One-Stop Store

Sugar—10-lb. bag—$4.70
Coffee—2-lb. can—$4.59
Turkey—76¢ lb.
Raisins—6 oz. box—69¢
Carrots—2 lb. for 89¢
Butter—$1.96 lb.
Cucumbers—38¢ each
Mixed nuts—12-oz. can—$3.99
Cereal—24-oz. box—$4.80
Apple juice—½ gallon—$1.82
Soft drinks—50¢ a can
Rolled roast—$2.59 lb.
Milk—65¢ a quart
Pineapples—2 for $1.89

NAME _____

Getting the Most for Your Money

Figure the best buy for each item. Write the letter for the column with the lowest price in the Best Buy column. Do your work on another piece of paper.

Item	A	B	C	Best Buy
1. Motor Oil	2 for $2.50	4 for $4.64	$1.29	B
2. Spark Plug	$1.14	4 for $3.96	8 for $7.36	
3. Glass Cleaner	3 for $3.87	2 for $2.98	$1.59	
4. Sponge	2 for $2.48	$1.39	4 for $4.88	
5. Paper Towels	4 for $2.76	94¢	2 for $1.42	
6. Detergent	2 lb. for $1.28	4 lb. for $1.88	6 lb. for $3.12	
7. Vinyl Top Cleaner	12-oz. can for $2.40	24-oz. can for $4.32	two 12-oz. cans for $4.56	
8. Car Wax	6-oz. can for $2.94	12-oz. can for $4.92	18-oz. can for $6.48	

	Item	A	B	C	Best Buy
9.		$6.96	2 for $12.98	$6.45	C
10.		2 for $7.00	8 for $24.00	4 for $13.00	
11.		3 for $24.66	2 for $19.00	$10.88	
12.		2 doz. for $26.00	1 doz. for $14.00	3 doz. for $36.00	
13.		$14.85	2 for $28.98	4 for $55.00	
14.		$19.89	$21.95	2 for $39.98	
15.		$13.99	3 for $37.50	2 for $25.50	
16.		$35.70	$37.50	2 for $73.00	
17.		2 for $24.96	$13.85	4 for $48.88	
18.		$29.99	4 for $99.92	2 for $56.00	

NAME _____

Below are some advertisements that are sent through
the mail. Write the price per unit on each blank. Then
write the name of the place that offers the lowest price.
Do your work on another piece of paper.

1.

CABLE TV
NEW – Living Room Theater
4 months for only $76.48!

Price per month $19.12

THE BEST IN CABLE
With UTV, you get
3 months for $52.32!

Price per month $17.44

Lowest-priced cable channel _____UTV_____

2.

BIKING MAGAZINE
Special!
12 issues – $22.20!

Price per issue _____

BIKER'S WORLD
Great Deal!
10 issues only $19.50!

Price per issue _____

Lowest-priced magazine _____

3.

SPA TIME HEALTH CLUB
New member Special
1st 4 months – just $91.00!

Price per month _____

FINE FITNESS CENTER
Join now!
Only $88.50 for 3 months

Price per month _____

Lowest-priced health center _____

4.

RENT OUR VIDEO TAPES
Summer Special
Any 4 video tapes – just $12.60

Price per video tapes _____

WE-MOVE VIDEO TAPES
Best deal ever
Your 1st 6 video tapes – $14.22!

Price per video tape _____

Lowest-priced rented video tapes _____

5.

ROCKY TAPE CLUB
Rock & Roll – $8.55
New Age – $7.95

LOW-DOWN MUSIC
Country – $7.45
Blues – $8.75
Jazz – $8.97

Total price $16.50

Divided by number of prices 2)$16.50

Average price $8.25

Total price $25.17

Divided by number of prices 3)$25.17

Average price $8.39

Lowest-priced tape dealer Rocky Tape Club

6.

BOOK WORLD BOOK CLUB
Hardbacks – $14.95
Paperbacks – $4.65

THE BOOK COMPANY
Hardbacks – $13.50
Paperbacks – $5.88

Total price _____

Divided by number of prices _____

Average price _____

Total price _____

Divided by number of prices _____

Average price _____

Lowest-priced book club _____

7.

GREEN GARDEN CENTER
Flower seeds – $.84
Vegetable seeds – $.76
Herb seeds – $.77

GROWING THINGS
Flower seeds – $.79
Vegetable seeds – $.81

Total price _____

Divided by number of prices _____

Average price _____

Total price _____

Divided by number of prices _____

Average price _____

Lowest-priced garden center _____

8.

BIG MEAL DINER
Lunch – $4.25
Dinner – $5.65

ETHEL'S EATERY
Lunch – $3.95
Dinner – $5.89

Total price _____

Divided by number of prices _____

Average price _____

Total price _____

Divided by number of prices _____

Average price _____

Lowest-priced restaurant _____

The Money Wheel

Start at the center and work between the spokes toward the rim. Follow the directions and fill in the blanks as you go. (Each answer is part of the next problem.)

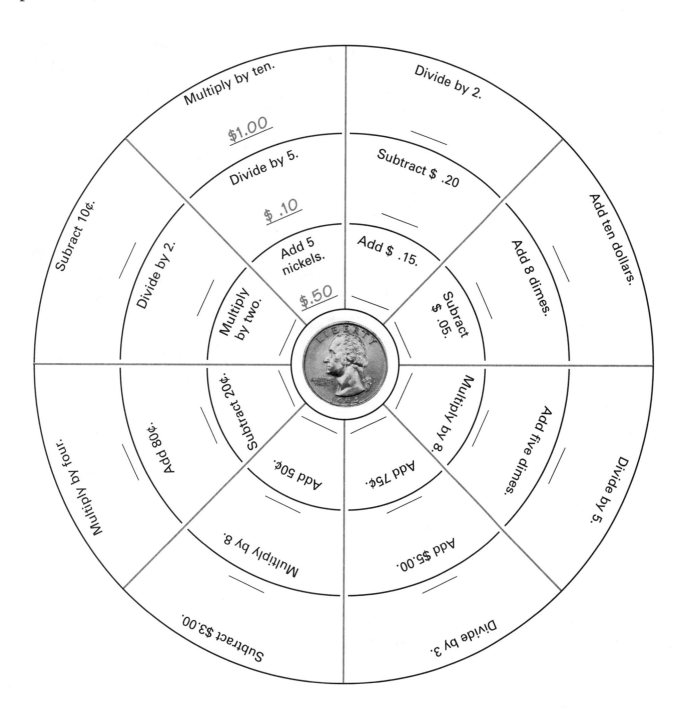

Add the answers around the rim of the wheel. What is the sum? _____

Finish this crossword puzzle by using the arithmetic you know. Use numbers in all your answers. Leave out decimal points, dollar signs, and cent signs.

Across

1. $10.00 − $6.06 = ?

3. 6 × $ .23 = ?

6. 288 ÷ 6 = ?

7. $1.44 ÷ 12 = ?

9. Penny

11. 4 × $12.73 = ?

13. 5 goes into 9095 how many times?

15. 48 ÷ 6 = ?

16. $1.05 ÷ 7 = ?

17. 8924 divided by 2 = ?

19. How many times will 9 divide into 135?

20. $20.00 − $10.98 = ?

21. Four cans of beans cost $1.40. How much does one can cost?

22. How many cents are in a half-dollar?

24. Cucumbers cost 24¢ each. How much would 3 cost?

25. 8 quarters, 4 dimes, and 2 pennies = ?

28. A bill with a picture of Lincoln.

29. Pumpkins cost 12¢/lb. How much will 11 lb. cost?

30. A belt costs $4.89. You have $2.50. How much more do you need?

31. You pay 75¢ for 3 lemons. How much does each cost?

Down

1. Pineapples cost $1.25 each. How much will 3 cost?

2. $.44 + $2.05 + $1.43 + $.27 = ?

4. Bananas are 5 lb./75¢. How much would 2 lb. cost?

5. Peppers cost 27¢ each. How much will 3 cost?

6. 34 × 129 = ?

8. 2366 − 151 = ?

10. You pay $5.00 for items costing 34¢, 18¢, 62¢, $2.54, and 43¢. Your change will be _____.

12. Large apples sell regularly for 30¢ each. How much money would you save if you bought 4 on sale at 4/$1.12?

13. 1641 − 219 = ?

14. Jeans cost $27.69. You pay $40.00. Your change is _____.

17. You pay $5.00 for paper that costs 93¢. Change = ?

18. 65 + 477 + 108 = ?

23. 7 × $3.22 = ?

25. If you get $7.11 in change from $10.00, the item cost _____.

26. 6)$12.90

27. 9)4743

Story Problem — Eating Out

Below is the menu in a sandwich shop. Read it carefully. Then answer the questions that follow.

The Sandwich House

Egg salad sandwich	$2.95	Fruit plate	$3.50
Ham and cheese sandwich	3.25	Vegetable soup	1.80
Tuna salad sandwich	3.15	Soup of the day	1.75
Turkey sandwich	3.25	Tossed green salad	1.90
Bacon, lettuce, and		Chef's salad	4.50
tomato sandwich	3.25	Milk	.75
Grilled cheese sandwich	2.75	Soft drinks	.85
Roast beef sandwich	3.45	Pie	1.95
Chicken salad sandwich	3.25	Ice cream	1.35

---

1. You order a tuna salad sandwich, soup of the day, milk, and a piece of pie. How much will your check be? _____ How much change should you get if you pay the cashier $8.00? _____

2. You and a friend order two ham and cheese sandwiches, two tossed green salads, and two milks. How much will your check be? _____ How much change should you get from $15.00? _____ How much will each of you pay if you divide the check in two? _____

3. You and two friends order three chicken salad sandwiches, three bowls of vegetable soup, three soft drinks, and three ice creams. How much will the check be altogether? _____ Dividing the check three ways, how much will each of you pay? _____ You pay the cashier $10.00 for your share. What should your change be? _____ Your friends pay $15.00 altogether for their share. What should their change be? _____

4. Five of you order the following: one bacon, lettuce, and tomato sandwich; three grilled cheese sandwiches; one egg salad sandwich; two bowls of soup of the day; and five milks. How much will the check be altogether? _____ What two bills could you give the cashier to get $3.30 in change? _____ If you divide the bill equally, how much will each of you pay? _____

5. You pick up the following order for a party you are having at home: four turkey sandwiches, two chicken salad sandwiches, five egg salad sandwiches, seven grilled cheese sandwiches, and two fruit plates. How much will the order cost? _____ If you pay the cashier four twenty-dollar bills, how much change should you get? _____ There were twenty people at the party. Did the food cost more or less than $3.00 per person? _____

6. Figure out these problems. Fill in the squares with your answers.

Order	Cost	Pay	Change	Divided	Cost Each
1 roast beef 1 ham and cheese 2 tossed green salads 2 soft drinks		$13.00		two ways	
2 turkey 2 fruit plates 4 milks 2 ice creams		$20.00		four ways	
2 tuna salad 3 chicken salad 4 vegetable soup 1 tossed green salad 1 milk 4 soft drinks			$.70		$5.86
4 grilled cheese 2 chef's salads 3 soup of the day 6 soft drinks 3 pie			$3.80	five ways	

Story Problem — The Art Fair

Julie makes leather belts to sell at art fairs. She keeps careful records of how much she spends to make the belts. She also keeps records of how much profit she makes when she sells the belts. Her profit is the difference between the cost of making the belts and the price she sells them for. Help Julie with her paperwork. Work the following problems and write your answers in the blanks.

1. Julie can buy 75 feet of leather for $99.00. How much does the leather cost per foot? _____ One belt takes three feet of leather. How many belts can she make from 75 feet of leather? _____ How much does the leather cost for each belt? _____

2. Julie can buy 25 belt buckles for $32.00. How much does each buckle cost? _____ How much does she spend altogether (leather and buckle) for each belt? _____

3. Julie sells her belts for $15 each. How much profit does she make for each belt that she sells? _____ It takes her 2 hours to make each belt. How much money does she make an hour for each belt she sells? _____

4. At the art fair, Julie sold 45 belts. How much money did she take in? _____ Subtract the cost of making the belts to find out how much profit Julie made at the fair. _____

Al works at the Metro Theater. He sells tickets for the afternoon and evening shows. The tickets sell for different prices for adults, for seniors (people 65 years old or older), and for children under 12. There are also different prices for the afternoon shows and the evening shows. These prices are shown below. Help Al work the following problems. Write your answers in the blanks.

	Afternoon	Evening
ADULTS	$4.75	$7.00
SENIORS	$4.25	$4.50
CHILDREN under 12	$4.50	$4.50

1. For an afternoon show, Al sold tickets to a family of two adults, one senior, and two children under 12. How much will their tickets cost altogether? _____ How much change will they get back if they give Al $25.00? _____

2. For an afternoon show, Al sold 22 adult tickets, 15 senior tickets, and 39 children tickets. How much money did he collect altogether? _____

3. One day, Al sold tickets to a group of 43 seniors. He collected $182.75. Was this for an afternoon or an evening show? _____

4. One evening, Al collected $133.00 in one hour for adult tickets. How many adults bought tickets? _____ He collected $126.00 for senior tickets. How many seniors bought tickets? _____ He collected $139.50 for children tickets. How many children bought tickets? _____ How many people bought tickets during that one hour?

_____

Story Problem — The State Fair

Five families are traveling to the state fair in Fair City. Each family lives in a different town and travels in a different way. The map shows where the families live and how far they travel. Help each family figure the cost of their trip. Use the information given about each family's trip to fill in the chart on page 122. Find the average cost per person by dividing the **money spent altogether** by the **number of people in the family.**

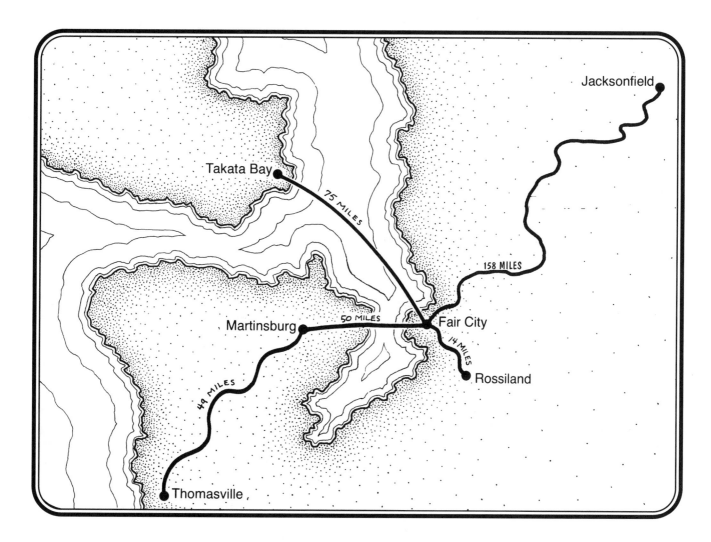

1. The Martin family drove their camper from Martinsburg to Fair City. They spent $10 on gas, $2 for a bridge toll, and $8.75 for a campsite. They also spent $36.25 for food for the trip. There are four people in the Martin family.

2. The Takata family took a boat from Takata Bay to Fair City. Tickets cost $15 each for adults, $9 each for children, and $12 each for seniors. There are two adults, two children, and two seniors in the Takata family.

3. The Rossi family traveled by bicycle from Rossiland to Fair City. Before they left, they bought two backpacks for $15.96 each. They also bought two new bicycle tires at $8.78 each. On the way to the fair, they bought four pounds of apples at 58¢ a pound. There are two people in the Rossi family.

4. The Thomas family took a bus from Thomasville to Fair City. Tickets cost $13.40 each for adults, $6.70 for children, and $12.50 for seniors. There are three adults, one child, and one senior in the Thomas family.

5. The Jackson family took a train from Jacksonfield to Fair City. Adult tickets cost $52.64 each. They can buy four children's tickets for the same price as one adult ticket. There are two children and one adult in the Jackson family. The trip cost 50¢ a mile.

	Martin	**Takata**	**Rossi**	**Thomas**	**Jackson**
Miles of travel					
Money spent altogether					
Cost per mile of trip					
Number of people in family					
Average cost per person					

6. Which family spent the most money altogether? _____ The least money altogether? _____ Which family's trip cost the most money per mile? _____ The least money per mile? _____ Which family spent the most per person? _____ The least per person? _____

NAME _____

Find the answers to these arithmetic problems.

1. $1.50
    − .36

2. $ .20
    + .17

3. $1.45
    + 1.70

4. $50.00
    − 4.45

5. $4.65
    × 9

6. $ .37
    × 6

7. $3.19
    − 1.68

8. 9)$ .99

9. $70.68
    − 23.35

10. $1.35
    × 3

11. $1.04
    − .94

12. 7)$1.05

13. $ .19
      .44
    + 2.43

14. $ 7.42
    × 13

15. $21.00
    − 8.17

16. $ .70
      .55
      .08
    + .28

17. $16.41
    − 2.26

18. $ .46
    × 19

19. 6)$6.36

20. $ .40
     5.21
      .16
    + 2.48

21. $40.80
    − 21.99

22. $13.16
      .57
     4.91
    + 22.48

23. $ 8.03
    × 12

24. 11)$13.20

25. $71.12
    − 3.39

26. 8)$67.04

27. $42.93
     6.55
      .76
     1.00
    + 29.37

28. $ 1.92
    × 49

29. $ 3.78
    × 23

30. $ 1.89
     34.44
     17.55
      .88
    + 1.13

31.   636
       × 52

32.   1040
       − 787

33.   2)924

34.   125
       × 39

35.   466
       978
     + 319

36.   3)5511

37.   577
       × 13

38.   7)2114

39.   8)5632

40.   961
       × 10

41.   5)2550

42.   394
       × 15

43.   8167
     − 4404

44.   4)2816

45.   303
       × 69

46.   9)4689

47.   12)3660

48.   214
       × 35

49.   11)2530

50.   2)1952

51.   118
       63
       905
       227
     + 19

52.   6)6096

53.   10)4580

54.   367
       × 24

Posttest II

1. You spend a Saturday morning at a garage sale. You buy a video tape for $4.95, a chair for $9.68, and a set of dishes for $13.29. How much do you spend altogether? _____

2. Four of your friends throw a party for your birthday. The bill for the cake, snacks, and drinks comes to $62.72. If your friends divide the bill by four, how much does each person have to pay? _____

3. You order T-shirts for the nine members on your basketball team. Each T-shirt costs $10.95. What is the total price for all the T-shirts? _____

4. Your best friend and his brother take you to the movies. The three tickets cost $16.50. Your friend gives the cashier $20.00. How much change does he get back? _____

5. Zappa's Music Store has a sale and takes $1.50 off the price of every tape. The tapes cost $8.97 each before the sale. You buy two tapes at the sale price. How much do you spend? _____

6. You and five members of your family get a job picking cherries. You pick 72 boxes of cherries altogether. The woman who owns the trees pays $2.50 for every box of cherries picked. If you divide the money evenly between all six family members, how much does each member get? _____

7. You buy three rolls of black and white film for $3.29 a roll, and five rolls of color film for $4.89 a roll. How much do you spend on film? _____

8. You and two friends make $90.87 selling cold drinks at a ball game. You use $42.63 to pay the bill for the drinks. Then you divide what's left over between the three of you. How much does each of you get? _____

9. Aster Auto Store has a sale on motor oil—eight cans for $7.12. Save-All's price is three cans for $2.97. Which store gives you the lowest price per can? _____

10. Corner's Market has eight-ounce bottles of grape juice for 72¢ a bottle. How much does the juice cost per ounce? _____

11. You're saving to buy a camera that costs $85.00. You have $52.35. How much more do you need? _____

12. You get paid $25.00 for doing yard work. You want to buy a CD for $11.25 and a watch for $13.40. Do you have enough money to buy both? _____

Multiplication Table

Knowing how to multiply will save you a lot of time when you are figuring out costs. Most people learn common multiplication facts by heart. One of the ways they learn is by using a multiplication table. Use this table to help you solve multiplication problems in this book.

✕	1	2	3	4	5	6	7	8	9	10	11	12
1	1	2	3	4	5	6	7	8	9	10	11	12
2	2	4	6	8	10	12	14	16	18	20	22	24
3	3	6	9	12	15	18	21	24	27	30	33	36
4	4	8	12	16	20	24	28	32	36	40	44	48
5	5	10	15	20	25	30	35	40	45	50	55	60
6	6	12	18	24	30	36	42	48	54	60	66	72
7	7	14	21	28	35	42	49	56	63	70	77	84
8	8	16	24	32	40	48	56	64	72	80	88	96
9	9	18	27	36	45	54	63	72	81	90	99	108
10	10	20	30	40	50	60	70	80	90	100	110	120
11	11	22	33	44	55	66	77	88	99	110	121	132
12	12	24	36	48	60	72	84	96	108	120	132	144

Table of Weights and Measurements

Knowing how to use different units of measurement will help you in figuring out costs. Use this table when you need to find out the price per unit of an item. You may want to learn some of the measurements by heart.

Weight

Ounce (oz.)	Pound (lb.)
16	1

Measurement

Inch (in.)	Foot (ft.)	Yard (yd.)	Mile
12	1		
36	3	1	
63,360	5,280	1,760	1

Liquid Measurement

Fluid Ounce (fl. oz.)	Cup	Pint (pt.)	Quart (qt.)	Half-gallon	Gallon
8	1				
16	2	1			
32	4	2	1		
64	8	4	2	1	
128	16	8	4	2	1